It's Always Sunny in Wrexham

ANDREW FOLEY JONES

ACKNOWLEDGEMENTS

To Wrexham FC, its wonderful fans, to Michael and Luke at Cool Thing, to Lina at Scenery Studios, to Kelly at KAB Productions, to Ian at Red Dog Promotions, to Sarah, Ianto, and Iolo, to my mum and my dad (for not turning off the A483), my sister and Mike (for taking me to some games I was too poor as a student to get to).

To my comrades over the years, at the games, Glyn, Colin, Stephen, Jason, and Alan for sharing the despair and the elation, to all at Fearless in Devotion, to everyone who has supported this great club, to Spencer Harris, Ryan Reynolds, Rob McElhenney, Humphrey Ker, and everyone in their team, and of course, to the players and the staff, for making this dream come true.

Prologue

This is a book about Wrexham A.F.C. It's also a book about life. If I'd have written this a couple of years ago, save for a few thousand die-hards, you wouldn't have been interested; chances are, you wouldn't even be reading this. You might have flicked past, to a more recognisable brand, a book about Real Madrid, Barcelona, Manchester City or Liverpool. You probably wouldn't have even heard of Wrexham, a town (now a city) in the northeast of Wales in the United Kingdom.

As you'll know from the stuff that's been in the media, on the news, on the Welcome to Wrexham documentary, in 2021, actors, writers, entrepreneurs, general good-guys, Ryan Reynolds and Rob McElhenney bought Wrexham Football Club that was then in the ownership of the supporters.

This is a book about dreams, about the underdog. It's written in the first person: that's me. It's set in 2030. That's seven years from now, as I sit, in my Wrexham shirt, pondering the future, reminiscing about the past.

Underdogs, in the main, don't succeed. They have their moments. But overall, they stay low in the pecking order. They have moments of fleeting glory, often in cup competitions. But then, after the cheap fizzy white wine has been poured ceremonially over the heads of managers who squirm like fools in giant dressing room baths, and the TV cameras disappear to the run of the mill news stories that make up the mundane every day, the football club returns to their day-to-day business of playing, inevitably with a hangover, maybe part literally, part metaphorically, where they lose to Ebbsfleet, or Dover, the following Tuesday evening.

I have been on this planet since 1972. I've supported Wrexham since 1979. I've witnessed what statisticians would term, 'limited successes' during this time. Let's think about it, I've (if you include any successes of the club, as mine personally), had two promotions, a couple of minor cup victories, and several giant killings in cup competitions, the latter of which are always delicious in their unexpectedness. It's been that sparse, I even claim avoiding relegation, as 'victories.'

So, what's the purpose of this book, of me writing about my experience. Is it piqued by the sudden interest in all things Wrexham FC related since 'the take-over' with a view to commercialising the opportunity, or is it a personal diary to maybe explain and therefore understand what an impact, supporting a lower league football club has on your life, on how it pans out, on your family and loved ones, friends, acquaintances, people who randomly share and pass through your life; a sort of therapy to help me understand myself as I slip into middle-age.

The reason for the book began with another story I was writing, fictional, non-Wrexham related, about a man who woke up in 2030 from a coma without any memory of his life beforehand. With the assistance of a psychiatrist and a wall of televisions (known as the 'Big TV,') they pieced together the decade he'd missed (it being written in the third person, the main protagonist being me), with a satirical lens on what I predicted was going to happen during the decade that was to come (the 2020s).

I started writing it in lockdown, surrounded, like everyone at the time, with the uncertainty that the pandemic brought, against the backdrop of family life (we had a two year old and a four week old when lockdown was announced) and a business I am a partner in; something that I had always done, writing articles for magazines, both to do with sport (Daily Post, Fearless in Devotion), and fiction (Tortoise, Concept for Living).

Although a lawyer by trade, I'd always written and had things published in magazines and the idea of the new book was, as I say, triggered by this strange new world. Some people started new businesses, I started foraging seaweed, writing the book, trying to keep the business going.

Lots of people didn't make it so without being melo-dramatic, from the misery and the death and the economic downturn, good things will hopefully emerge. The way society operates, the balance between work and life. The way we treat each other.

Despite the pandemic being over, we are as I write this, still in uncertain times; there is political unrest, a scepticism towards those who rule and govern, a truly monstrous war in Ukraine. If there's ever a time that needed a good news story, it's now.

For some context, I'd also happened to act as a lawyer to Wrexham Football Club for several years prior to the takeover. Spencer Harris, the former CEO who was at the helm prior to Ryan and Rob, was often heroically, steering the ship, alongside a demanding day job, with the assistance of others who also had day jobs and who were helping run a football club, simply for the bloody love of it.

I'll talk about it more later, but there's an often-irrational love that underpins the loyalty surrounding why we blindly follow a football club. The word 'fan' it is often forgotten, derives from the word 'fanatic.' These people, from the CEO, through to the board of directors, to the office staff, the stewards, the turnstile operators, the club mascot; they all give their time, their sweat, their tears, because of their love of the club. And in return, you get perhaps a feeling, of worth, of being part of something, a belonging. And I don't mean this is a football tribe, hooligan context, which I will touch upon later.

I met Spencer, through my friend Colin, who I met on a street in Chester (our arch-rivals) who also helped the club in various guises. Spencer, on discovering I was lawyer, asked if I was happy to give my time and my 'expertise.' I said 'of course, it would be an honour' and of course, it genuinely was.

The funny thing is, when you're a lawyer, you specialise in certain things. I for instance, do what is classed as 'commercial law' which involves the legal work associated with the sale and purchase of businesses, property, land. If you asked me to do your divorce, make you a will, sue someone, get you compensation for a bump in your car, find you a loophole for a speeding offence (usually from the unmarked car on the A483 on the Gresford turnoff), I wouldn't have a clue.

People don't always realise this. They think, generically, you know everything to do with the law. But the point is I suppose, from Spencer and the club's perspective, I had some knowledge and I'd know a person who did know more about something that I didn't.

I quickly got to know Spencer. I was lucky. I was in the background helping when the need arose. Spencer was, to continue the marine analogy, at the helm, visible at the front of this massive tanker that is Wrexham Football Club, steering it through troubled waters, riddled with vast ice bergs, vicious sharks, giant octopus, with an appetite to bring this ship crashing down through the depths. I'll keep the metaphor going through this tale. I don't like water, especially dark water that I can't see through which is where it probably comes from.

We've had some hilarious moments, some moments of sheer complexity, some decisions that were genius, some inevitably, glaringly incorrect. It's how running a business goes. It's how being a human being goes. A horrible boss I once had when I was a trainee solicitor said the 'man who makes no mistakes, makes no decisions.'

Putting aside for the moment that this man was a monster, and a slave driver, and someone who had no concern whatsoever for my welfare, looking back (and I was in no way what could be called 'a snowflake'), this was a fleeting moment of wisdom and the one thing I took away from my two years of misery with him as my 'boss.'

It's correct, if you make no decisions, you will make no mistakes. If you want that kind of life, you are destined to never be, prone to pardon my parlance, 'fucking up.' It's safe. You can trundle (Lee Trundle?) along; you might be prone to criticising others who have taken the decision, consciously or otherwise, to make decisions and thereby, be susceptible to making the occasional 'fuck up.'

I'm not breaching any confidentiality when I say, sometimes, it's like you put your finger in the air after licking it, and trying to guess which way the wind is blowing. And that guess is the act of making a decision. Think about it for a moment. Running a football club is something of a particular nuanced business to run. For those of you out there who run your own business, I'm guessing, it might be a law firm, as in my case, a plumbing business, a pub, a restaurant, an engineering business, a cleaning company, a doctor's surgery, an optician, a company offering financial advice.

You get the idea, there are a plethora of different businesses out there, all of which offer their own challenges, their own skill set, their own demands, risks, rewards. My occupational psychologist friend Colin will have much more technical input to offer and if you want his details, message me.

This business of a football club, especially when you have no knowledge of running one before; no training, no qualifications, no course, no teachers, lecturers, mentor's, to help you learn the ropes, it's just you and some other volunteers, who have to use their life experiences and common sense in a compressed period of time to make far reaching and often monumental decisions which affect the club and everyone involved in it, from the players, the paid staff, and most of all, the fanatics out there, the majority of which have no idea or care, of what is going on behind the scenes.

Their only concern is what happens on a Saturday afternoon, a Tuesday evening, when they go perhaps for a couple of pints before the game, then full of beer and hope and expectation, trot along to the stadium in Wrexham or wherever we may be playing for the particularly loyal supporter who follow their club away from home, 'on the road.'

The Ranken-file supporter who might make up most of the demographic of a football clubs fan base, especially in the lower leagues, just want their team to win, to play well, to climb the leagues, be successful; maybe as an aside, to play beautiful football.

Anyhow, back to the story; amidst the fiction, is interwoven with some fact. Some anecdotes, memories of things to do with life, football and inevitably, Wrexham FC. There are clips about the famous events that everyone remembers, the Arsenal giant killing, the European trips, a couple of promotions - but for me, it's more the random, the ad hoc, that resonate, that make me recall, make me replay, make me cry, make me smile and everything in between.

There's the punch in the face at Scunthorpe on a cold Tuesday night, the iconic missed FA Cup Replay because my eye got caught by a girl on a train, a board room pre-match dinner in Barrow in Furness, a pint of cider in Chesterfield that made me hallucinate, a Mexican on a plane to Qatar who thought I was Paul Mullin, my mate who looked like a former Chester Chairman, who attended a game when supporters thought this awful human being was trying to buy our club, a mate of my dad who was linesman against Bristol Rovers whose decision lost us the game and my dad a friend.

Football and life run in parallel. There are things that happen which contrary to what a legendary Liverpool manager said, are clearly more important than football. There are those pivotal moments that humankind holds close to their hearts and soul: birth, death, love, respect.

But perhaps it's not that simple. One isn't more important than the other. They co-exist, they happen in parallel. You lose a loved one and at the same time you beat Middlesborough in an FA Cup tie, and within that 90-minute bubble, you don't think about what you've lost, the all-encompassing grief, the desperate feeling of loss and that life will never be the same again.

And that is perhaps what football is, in a simple snapshot. It's a thing, a distraction from every day, the shit, the joy, the loss, the euphoria, the promotion, the death, the love, the birth, the redundancy; all the things that happen, every minute, every hour, every day, every week, every month, every year - the things that make up a life and an existence.

This isn't a textbook about life, or football or Wrexham FC. There are plenty of publications out there which tell such stories much better than I ever could. This is my personal version, reflection, anecdote, memory, history, and ultimately a prediction or whatever you want to call it.

It's prone to criticism, review, comment. It's exposing, putting something out there. Like putting on a kit and playing in front of a crowd or writing a tune and playing in front of an audience, telling a poem at an open mic night.

Anyone who creates and puts it out there, I applaud you all. You should all be given credit for taking the risk, for trying to entertain, even if it doesn't, please all the people, all the time.

The rest of this story is fiction, well for now, it is fiction, as it's set in the future. It's me waking up in 2030 and finding out what's happened to society, to Wrexham, to Wales, the UK, the wider world; a prediction, sometimes satirical, sometimes, plain daft, a forecast if you like of what might happen in the rest of this unprecedented, crazy decade that is the 2020s.

It's a strange genre, I accept, part fact, part fiction, about a fifth level non-league football club, about society. What I predict will happen when I've woken up from the coma in 2030 might sound right here, right now, outlandish, something born out of far-fetched fiction, a silly plot in a superhero movie, an episode in some long running sit com.

But the thing about fiction, about dreams, about the underdog, is sometimes it does come true, the underdog does, on occasion, have its day; fact can often be stranger than fiction. And maybe, that is what this is ultimately about. It's a good news story. It's the hope that in parallel to your football club rising through the leagues, life can get better, that we may get to see a fairer and happier future, socially, economically, and politically.

Enjoy the ride. One thing is for sure, it's going to be bumpy. We are all, as they say, fearless in devotion. COYR.

IT'S ALWAYS SUNNY IN WREXHAM

Some of the following may actually have happened...

May 2030

So, you think 2020 was a shitstorm. Try this, it's 2030, and you wake up in a room with no memory of how you got there. Sat by your bed is famous psychiatrist, Dr Paskin, and a Big TV fills the wall opposite, playing images of stuff that appears to have happened during the 2020s whilst you've been out of the game in a decade long coma. Oh, and I suppose I should mention after a couple of weeks of recuperation, I have visitors: Hollywood A-Listers, Ryan Reynolds and Rob McElhenney.

The first thing I need to explain is this all did really happen. I'm writing it at the end, like a ridiculous self-obsessed diary written by a teenager who just wants to make their mark, ink a tattoo, make a difference in the world. The only thing is, I'm not a teenager. I'm nearly sixty for fuck-sake, chatting to these people, talking about the meaning of life, bandwagons, lifers, the offside rule, whether it's ever socially acceptable to wear Crocs.

They'll try and explain how it was I got to be laid out on my backside in a coma for the last decade, how it is that I'm now sitting here, in a football stadium, my lowly fifth tier non-league football club about to compete in the biggest game in their history.

They'll be telling me how they decided to buy a football club, something I've supported for fifty years, how they dared to dream big, how they devised a plan to climb the sporting pyramid, to build and run something sustainably, with a community focus, to bring on new supporters to supplement the existing fan base; to make Wrexham F.C. into an internationally recognised brand, to ultimately take a non-league minnow right up to the Premier League.

They might be trying to explain what has happened over the last decade is a thing of beauty, a script right out of Hollywood, a super-hero looking out for the little guy, a drama the best screenwriter couldn't make up, a sprinkling of stardust being thrown over the town.

They might try and explain why players were clamouring to come out of retirement to join the cause, how they set up an academy so home-grown players would come through the system and want to play for their local club.

They might want to explain the other crazy stuff that's happened this decade; the fall of a monarchy, the assassination of Donald Trump and Vladimir Putin, the Tories falling out of favour, the breakup of the United Kingdom, the world becoming a fairer place.

My initial reaction is that I must still be in a coma, having absurd dreams. I touch the arm of Ryan Reynolds and it appears real. I want to pinch Rob McElhenney, but it might come across weird. I want to ask a myriad of questions; 'how did all this happen, why me, why Wrexham, and again, why Wrexham?'

"Watch the documentary" says Ryan "oh, and all the shit on YouTube" adds Rob, "yeah, there's a lot of it" says Rob. "It's all explained on there, oh and there's loads of press from all over the planet, which will give you the full picture."

I look down. I'm wearing Crocs, a pair of tracksuit bottoms with Macron written across the leg and the Wrexham F.C. badge, my initials beneath it. I've also got a training jacket with the words Aviation Gin and Betty Buzz on the front.

We're sat in a corporate suite high above the stand I used to sit in, on the Mold Road, the main thoroughfare into Wrexham. It's exquisite, pictures on the wall of various moments of matches, pivotal moments in the history of the club, posters of Deadpool movies and It's Always Sunny in Philadelphia. It's plush, without being pretentious.

There's a coffee machine in the corner and a man with a big quiff and a posh English voice, sounding like Louis Theroux, introducing himself, shaking my hand, asking if I'd like to partake in a beverage. "A flat white would be great," I say, "in a takeaway cup and extra hot, if possible." "Of course," he responds and a minute later he hands me the cup. It tastes fantastic, a million miles away from the terrible shit they used to serve back in the day. If the improvement in the coffee is a metaphor for improvements in the entire football club, then bring it on, we've gone from Maxwell House instant to the best coffee in the world.

"All in the detail" he smiles. "I completely agree, it's all about the detail, the culture of the club from top to bottom, from the program sellers to the ball boys, right through to your centre forward, it's all about the minutiae."

It helps of course that we have the budget, the exposure. If the supporters trust who previously had custody of the football club had wasted money on great coffee, the head of Spencer Harris (the CEO), would have rolled. These things always need to be looked at in context. But still, Humphrey is to be commended for his choice of coffee, on his appreciation of the finer detail.

The view across the stadium is incredible. I take in the vista of the town below (it's technically now a city, Humphrey reminds me), the grid of streets I recognise from before, the line of poplars opposite from where we're sitting, the rolling hills and fields beyond. Humphrey says, "it must be a lot to take in, there must be a lot of memories here."

I nod, adding, "the thing is, I can point to every corner of this ground and tell you what score it was when I sat here, there, who scored, who the opposition were, what I was doing in my life, whether I was happy, indifferent, anxious, despairing over some decision, grieving over a lost love, the death of a friend. I can tell you the people I sat by and who the substitutes were that day. I can tell you the mood my dad was in, whether his business was going well or to shit or somewhere in between."

Humphrey smiles warmly. Rob has a tear in his eye. Ryan is trying to get to an awkward itch through his Deadpool outfit; there's a design flaw right there. Danny DeVito, on video link on the Big TV on the wall of the suite, is drinking from a bottle of Bootlegger Lager by Wrexham Lager. He's with David Beckham, Barack Obama, Lady Gaga, Prince Harry, who collectively, in the background, wish me good luck.

It's not your run-of-the-mill group of people I normally watch a game with. Glyn, Colin, Stephen, Jason, Alan, you're truly great friends, and I've loved watching the games with you, especially during the shit times when we needed some dark humour to see us through, but you cannot deny, this is left field.

I continue my monologue to this group of absurdly famous onlookers. I'm not intimidated at all and perhaps it's the ten years of being mute, in my comatose state, but I feel the need to impart some fact, some history, some insider knowledge to these A-Listers, who appear to have brazenly jumped upon the Wrexham F.C. bandwagon during the 2020s.

"I can point you to the taps that throw out the scolding water, the hand dryers that spill out freezing air which wouldn't dry you in a million years. I can tell you about the girl in the snack counter who'll always give you the wrong change, the woman who will always put the lid on the coffee so it slips when you take a sip (I recall scolding my balls during the half time interval in a home victory over Ebbsfleet United).

I can tell you about the turnstile operator who takes forever to scan your ticket and wants to chat about the roadworks on the A483 when you're running late and just want to get your seat, the program seller who has a mother with dementia, the barmaid in the Saith Seren who really doesn't want to be a barmaid at all, the mascot who loves pretending to be a man-sized dragon come match day, the kid who yearns for the return of Rockin' Robin."

"The old mascot?" asks Rob. "Exactly" I respond, impressed by his level of knowledge; this is nuanced stuff. "And don't forget Robin's girlfriend" adds Rob "who used to cycle in on a bike" laughs Humphrey. "What was her name again?" he asks. "Tina Turfit" says David Beckham through the screen of the TV on the wall, "axed in 2001 to be replaced with Wrex the Dragon." "I remember him having a fist fight with Ollie the Owl, the Sheffield Wednesday mascot back in the day" I add, "maybe that had something to do with it." "A sad day" adds Barack Obama, "I'm just delighted you've brought them both back."

"You see, this place is not just a football ground, it's not just a place to come and watch a game of football. It's way more than that. It grabs you and takes you inside. It fucks with your head, it makes you wake in the night and you're not sure why there's a knot in your stomach, why you wake grumpy on a Sunday morning, and you realise it's the stark realisation that you're pissed off because you lost 3-2 to Maidenhead United. It's irrational. It's insane. It is absurd. It grabs you by the balls and twists them so tight, you think your eyeballs are going to pop out of your head" I explain.

Rob, Ryan, and Humphrey hugged me. It's a four-way monster hug. On the video link, the famous onlookers are joining in. I can feel the love squeezing out of us like a massive tube of love paste. "It's crazy" I add, "that it can be so evil and gorgeous, so exhilarating, it can be the greatest drug on earth, you can love every moment of hating it. I hope you're not going to disrespect the past, please don't ever make us play in blue, or forget pivotal moments in our history. I mean, we all love a Hollywood story, a sprinkling of stardust, but don't ever forget the essence of the club, the town, the culture of the people of this place."

They glance sideways at each other. I might be paranoid, but it feels a bit awkward or 'awks,' as the youngsters, I understand, now say. Ryan mentions the away kit is a pale blue, but it really was well received, and we did used to play in blue back in the day. I don't say anything. The silence hangs like a fog in the air, on a cold, winter morning.

There's still an hour or so until kick off. The stadium is filling up. Rob and Ryan say they've got so much they want to ask me to talk about. They understand way more than they did all those years ago when they took over, but that they're still light years behind people like me who have been immersed in this world, all their lives. I have fifty odd years on them. That's a lot of frustration, disappointment, false dreams, injury time defeats, shocking signings, and terrible coffee to have built up like the magma that seeps up from a volcano after millions of years. I'm ready to vent. I'm ready to erupt.

They seem to have learnt a lot about the culture of football during their tenure of ownership. They appear authentic, engaged and beyond the realms of celebrity and gimmick. It feels better than having 'oil' money built up from corrupt regimes who treat human beings with contempt, or some local 'businessmen' with bloated egos, a penchant for fake tans and an appetite for the development of real estate on land that should only be used for the local community.

I remember such characters from the past. Narcissistic human beings, exploiting opportunity, disrespecting the fabric of the community. If you're reading this, shame on you. May your actions haunt your sleep, you greedy, vile bastards.

Then the fans stepped up. Incredible, selfless people who brought in life savings, deeds for their homes, pocket money, a display of everything that is wonderful about the human spirit, an antidote to the poisonous individuals who had attempted to ruin the football club.

The fans took over, became custodians, so that it could never fall victim to the asset-stripping chancers who might be circling like sharks around a stricken boat.

It would have been beautiful to have succeeded under the fan-owned model but in the modern world of football this is impossible. It's a romantic notion but one which will only end in heartache.

"The fan ownership model should not be viewed as failure" I point out, "it should be regarded as a steppingstone to where we are now; without it, none of this" I say, spreading out my arms, "would have happened. Spencer Harris and the others that ran the show during that era need to be congratulated. Without them, we wouldn't be here today."

They all nod in agreement. "Spencer was pivotal in this" says Rob. "Absolutely" agree Ryan and Humphrey. "Those who have ever uttered a bad word in his direction are weasels" adds Danny DeVito, winking on the video link.

They want to know how I coped supporting a team who had 'limited'

16

success. I smile. They've said it in as respectful a way as they could. It's true, if I had the stats, my win rate as a fan would be woeful. Maybe I'll try and work it out one day.

There may be someone doing a PHD in it right now. The impact the success or failure of your team has in your life. If you support a successful team, do you have more chance of being successful in your life, mirroring the success of the team you support? Or does it work the other way round? Do years of disappointment spur you on to better yourself in other aspects of your life?

"I'm not sure," I say, "but what I do know, is the way you react to defeat is important. It's important when you lose a lot. When you're invested and there's no way of retracting that. It's not like taking a coat back to River Island because it doesn't fit right, or you realise now in a different light that the colour just isn't you and it goes shit with your favourite jeans. No, you're stuck with this. It's indelibly stained in your soul, an irreversible tattoo on the nape of your back, an invisible crest of the club on your aching heart."

Ryan wipes a tear from his eye. I continue, not stopping for anyone.

"So, you must get used to learning to lose. Develop a coping mechanism. Try and take it with good grace. Return home from the game or turn off the radio or switch off the stream and resist kicking the cat, speak kindly to your loved ones, play with your kids, don't be a sulky twat - it's not a good look, even when it wrecked your gut, when a referee has fucked you over with a decision, when you feel everything is stacked against you. You need to learn this from day one. It's not in any textbooks. You've got to work it out yourself. It'll save you a lot of heartache and arguments.

I don't want to appear all evangelical, but people forget sometimes that in sport, there are two teams. Yours and the opposition. Both are trying to achieve a result. People, typically the most extreme form of fanatic, forget that the opponent is also trying to carve out a result, they're not just going to roll over and let you win. The result is that unless you're the Invincibles of Arsenal, you must accept defeat and deal with it.

17

This burden grows as you become more successful. We must learn to manage this, manage the expectations of these fanatics. They will otherwise become a burden, moaning, entitled Frothers who will only serve to hinder, hold us back, and retard our progress."

I've delivered this monologue in the new private urinal just through from the suite, which has been built at the top of the Mold Road Stand, now sponsored by coffee shop The Jaunty Goat who now supplies the coffee, after a rigorous tender process.

Ryan, squeezing out the remnants of the last strain of his urine, falling in slow motion like droplets of rain or a speeding bullet in one of his movies, moves to the washbasin where we both lather for twenty seconds, viewing a poster for a concert in the summer of 2030 for The Arctic Monkeys, supported by The Alarm and The Declan Swans.

The urinal is Armitage Shanks, the basin, Twyford's, both iconic and exemplary objects of sanitaryware. As Humphrey says, it's all in the minutiae.

"Why Wrexham?" It's something I must ask. It's a horribly awful, obvious, clichéd question. Whichever way you look at it. I've got the coma card to play, which gives the question a little more legitimacy. I'm pretty sure as I exert the words from my mouth, that it's been asked a million times before.

"You haven't seen the documentary yet have you" grins Rob, patiently, understandably passing the question on. "Yeah, we talk quite a bit about it there, you know, amongst other stuff" deadpans Deadpool. "It's a pretty decent show, award-winning, you should put it on your watch list."

"Maybe after Breaking Bad, and Stranger Things, and maybe give that Lost a go" adds Rob "always baffled me that one." "Don't think some things are meant to be understood" offers Ryan "they're made without a conclusion, just to make us think and consider."

On the video link, Danny DeVito winking, chirps in with "highly profound Mr. Superhero. Maybe your next Deadpool can be a little less wham, bam, boom and a little more conceptual." Ryan responds sharply "come back to me when you've had a single hit movie, you little shit."

Ignoring their banter, I ask another well-worn question: "Were there any other clubs you thought of buying before Wrexham?"

Rob and Ryan exchange a look with Humphrey who flicks back his gloriously glossy and thick fringe from his forehead and points out: "Well, yeah there were a couple on the short list."

"Oh yeah, like who?" I ask.

"Hartlepool United" says Rob.

"Yeah, and Grimsby" adds Humphrey.

"Shit" I say, "so, why didn't they make the cut?"

"Have you been to Hartlepool or Grimsby?" asks Humphrey.

"Well, yes, both" I respond, thinking of a couple of footballing trips made in my near history. "Proper working towns. I thought that was one of your USP's?"

"Yeah, it is, but they lacked the soul and community feel of Wrexham" says Humphrey.

"And they're not in Wales" I add winking.

"That's very true" says Humphrey, "and in all seriousness, that did add another dimension to the decision-making process."

"Well, thank fuck for that" I add, offering my cup of coffee as a gesture of cheers which they all reciprocate chinking glasses, declaring "to Wrexham."

During my post-coma recuperation, I've caught up on the nine Deadpool's and countless episodes of It's Always Sunny in Philadelphia. It leads us seamlessly into our next topic of conversation. "I remember Deadpool" I say to Ryan, "I mean, from back in the day."

He seems to be waiting for a critique, at least some form of gesture to indicate my view, as I get the impression, he does care what I think.

"And you liked it?" asks Ryan.

"Yeah, I didn't know what to expect as I'm not a fan of the superhero genre apart from the serious gems, Batman, Joker etc, and I had no idea it was a spoof thing. It was seriously well done. Clever, witty, satirical. Very fucking funny, I'll be honest, I wasn't a massive fan of the sequel, but I've enjoyed, what is it" I say, unfolding my fingers, counting each subsequent release, moving onto thumbs as we reach double digits.

"Remind us all, what you are up to now Ryan" smirks Rob, pointing at a movie release picture, framed on the wall opposite where we sit in our corporate suite.

"Ten" says Rob.

"Fucking ten" says Ryan "that's what you call milking the fuck out of it. Have some fucking respect for yourself, for your art, man" says Rob, trying to stifle some laughter.

Ryan retorts, "and this from the man who's what, up to Series 27 of It's Always Sunny in Philadelphia and, you choose to employ your wife, you sad bastard."

"At least there's no Green Lantern 2" quips Rob, retaliating with a forced burst of laughter whilst sticking a finger in the direction of Ryan Reynolds.

"I'm an artist man" add Rob "you're a fucking clown."

"Yeah, but a very successful clown" offers Humphrey.

"There is that" accepts Rob, "there is that."

Humphrey suggests we head for a pint in The Turf, the iconic public house that has forever been part of the fabric of the football club. I used to go there drinking orange squash as my dad and his mates had a pre-match pint. I then, once able to obtain a fake I.D., used to go there myself, with my mates; it was a massive part of our day. It's an iconic place, intrinsically linked to the football club and the town. The landlord Wayne and his wife, Shelley, I recognise from my pre-coma days and like me, they've aged slightly but look well. I ordered a Guinness and everyone else has pints of Wrexham Lager.

I tell Rob and Ryan that they really should be applauded for some of the improvements they've brought to the football club. This is on the proviso that I've not attended any form of match for ten years and this perhaps puts me in a decent position to judge, to reflect on the changes that have been made.

Rob's reaction is one of intrigue. As they've been part of this journey over the past decade, the improvements are gradual, evolving and they might not be as stark as they are to me. He says he's proud of this and asks me to list, in no order, the things that have got better since they took over the reins of the club. I oblige, in no order.

Better Players: I've not seen a game apart from some clips on the Big TV, but to be where we are now in the footballing pyramid, it's an obvious one but the standard of player, coach, infrastructure, it makes for a better team, a better style of football, better entertainment, and better results. I recall some of the stuff I watched in the past, during non-league, when we couldn't compete with other teams, with greater resources. It became a thing of tedium; it just wasn't entertaining any more.

Streaming: I explain that for many of the new supporters, they'll never know of a time before being able to watch a game in real time, on a live stream. Without sounding like an old turnip, it wasn't long ago when there wasn't even radio coverage, let alone watching it live. I remember a thing called CLUBCALL, back in the 1980s - a phone number which was charged at premium rate, and it allowed you to listen to a game for an allotted period. After racking up a bill that my dad couldn't quite fathom, it was claimed that it had been caused by my mother calling her newly emigrated friend in New Zealand.

This ruse successfully enabled me to safely take in the last 15 minutes of each game, secretly listening on the phone in my parents' bedroom whilst they watched TV downstairs. My deception caught up with me when I inadvertently screamed in delight as I celebrated an injury time winner over Carlisle United. The result was two-fold. My dad nearly hit me with my Taid's (Welsh for grandfather) walking stick, thinking I was an intruder and secondly, the colossal phone bill was caused not by a careless mother but rather by my footballing obsession.

Match Day Experience: The atmosphere at the stadium and in the city is on a different level. The Mold Road Stand is the only one that has remained the same as when I last attended a game (apart from the new corporate suite from where we view the game). The other two stands match the new stand that was built where the previous standing area known as The Kop used to be, behind the goal on our right-hand side.

History: Rob and Ryan say they met with my parents, my partner, my kids soon after the accident and so knew a little bit about me. They say they've heard mixed things about Rhyl, that Prestatyn has a slightly better reputation. I explain that when you're from somewhere you can slag it off. It's like when you give your mum a hard time; it's alright, just about for you to do it, but no one else right.

North Wales is like that. Like most places, it's a mixed bag, a melting pot of industrial wasteland, deprived housing estates, dead end seaside towns, slag heaps silhouetting disused and decaying machinery and then the paradoxically stunning landscape, Snowdonia, the coastline, Anglesey, lush rolling hills, friendly villages, and towns.

And there are those seaside places again - they can be magical in the summer when they come alive. It's the winter when they can be desolate, windswept places.

Overall, it's a beautiful place alright, carved out by a rough natural force, a hard edge, tinged with honesty, integrity, and respect. Being Welsh adds another dimension to the place. It makes you feel different, not English, proud to be part of a minority, even if there are sometimes more English people living in your town than indigenous Welsh.

You see, I explain to them all, I grew up here in a seaside town where the tourists came mainly from the northwest towns and cities of England. They came to our caravan parks, our budget hotels, the sprawling holiday park they call Pontins, a prisoner of war style camp where Scousers and Mancs would holiday in glorious tribal technicolour, the all-day drinking sessions, family talent shows, often ending in abject violence, bar brawls spilling out into the summer evenings. It was a paradise of sorts and was my playground as a young boy, sneaking through the barbed wire security fences to learn about life and girls and cheap lager and the fruit machines in the amusement arcades.

People came here on holiday. They thought it was ace, better than their grids of terraced towns where everyday life played out and where life was mundane and hard going. The promenade and the sandy beach and the dunes where lovers could get lost in the cleavage of the bosoms of fine sand and the amusement arcades and the crazy golf and the candy floss and ice cream and the shitty everyday was for two weeks, forgotten.

This was of course before the days of cheap flights and the package holiday, when going abroad was as likely as going into space on a rocket with Richard Branson or Elon Musk. Prestatyn was paradise not only to these holiday makers but also to my parents, working class, my mother's family from the Welsh island of Anglesey, my father from an immigrant family from Kilkenny, Ireland, both settling in this place, sixty miles west of Liverpool, two hundred and forty miles north of London, some eighty years ago.

I spent the first two years of my life in the nearby town of Rhyl, a rough place where ex criminals took over the splendid Victorian hotels now divided into bedsits as the tourists swapped Rhyl for Torremolinos or Benidorm as Freddy Laker brought cheap aviation to the UK.

We then grew up in a new build housing estate in the suburbs of Prestatyn, safe and conservative, playing football and cricket in our street with the other kids, back in the 1970s, before technology brought at first, basic computers, the mobile phone, the internet, and social media.

This place was unremarkable in many ways. It was white. It was working class. It was a back water where not much ever really happened and as the Del Amitri song goes, 'the needle goes back to the start of the song, and we all go along like before.'

But it was safe, and it was home, and it was honest and proud. Thirty-eight miles along the coast and a bit inland was the industrial mining town of Wrexham, a place I don't think I'd ever had reason to visit, despite its relative closeness geographically; that was, until the winter of 1979, a visit that would, without being a drama-queen, end up blasting open my world.

I wanted to be a footballer from as far back as I can remember. I recall a photograph of me in a full Wrexham kit, the red Adidas strip of the mid-1970s. I was carrying a cup, something from the Rhyl and District Cup around 1978.

My dad had been a semi-professional footballer, a railway man, then a door-to-door insurance salesman for the Prudential, then fell into estate agency. He taught me the lure of the beautiful game. To keep it simple. Play the way you're facing. Savour possession. Don't fear starting again.

I was going to be a footballer. It was all I wanted to be. I was only ever going to play for Wrexham FC. I was only ever going to win the First Division as the top league was called back then, with Wrexham, and of course, the World Cup, as the captain of Wales. Back then, Wrexham were in the old Division 3 (now league 1) and Wales were ranked behind Swaziland and the Faroe Islands.

There's a heavy knock on the front door of The Turf that has been closed now to the public with kick off so close. It brings me out of my melancholy. One of the doormen checks outside and comes back and whispers something into Rob's ear. Rob relays the information he has received.

"Hugh Jackman is outside with his crew" says Rob, "he says he'd like to come in for a pre-match pint. Shall we let him in?"

Ryan looks to Rob, Rob looks to Humphrey, Humphrey looks to me.

"No fucking way" says Ryan, "no fucking way."

"Do you not think it might be a good thing to do?" suggests Humphrey.

Ryan is quite clear. "No fucking way, he's a fucking fanny. He's not coming in" reiterates Ryan.

The doorman disappears and tells Hugh Jackman, dressed as his character, Wolverine, arch-rival of Reynolds' Deadpool, that he isn't coming in. He's the new owner of a rival football club who we'll be playing today in the biggest game of our history; it's surreal, but more of that later.

Everyone is quiet. There's a feeling of foreboding. I ask them how it was I got to be in a coma in the first place. It was quickly becoming an elephant in the corner, even this early in our absurd relationship.

Wayne looks down to the Guinness tap. His wife grabs some Scampi Fries. Rob plays with a beer mat. Everyone seems to be looking elsewhere, a section of wall, some silent airspace. Eye contact is nil. There's a palpable feeling of awkwardness. Nobody wants to address my question.

I gather these are the possibilities:

I got punched in the head by the Hungarian lad at five-a-side. He'd held a grudge against me, for ages, for some banter about 'goulash' that he honestly took out of context. I love Hungary and Goulash and Budapest; to think I would be critical, racist even, is abhorrent.

Or is it that I got caught up in some football violence over at Oldham Athletic, when having sold the away end out in 12 minutes, I decided to sit on my hands in the 'home' end? I hadn't banked on a 97th minute penalty to win it, my body lurching skywards as your knee might when hit by a doctor's hammer. Like a pack of wolves, hundreds of men, dressed mainly in Stone Island, many wearing goggles, might have swarmed over me, like in a Zombie mini-series, beating me to a Welsh pulp.

Or I caught some bad infection after having my appendix out, discharging myself two hours after the operation so that I could make the home game against Dorking Athletic. I might have felt very cold, despite my Wrexham Beach towel that I had covered myself in, to try and keep warm. The wound caused by the key-hole surgery might have been seeping and only Glyn's wife, Sue's milky coffee from a flask, made any in-roads to keeping away the chill. It felt like I was on an Antarctic expedition, and I'd been in a fight with an elephant seal (surprisingly strong and aggressive).

There are other possibilities that I haven't even thought of. I look around the room. It's quiet apart from the stuff that's coming out of the jukebox, some Smashing Pumpkins low drone from the 1990s, the background sound of football noise, Hugh Jackman's people banging on the window shouting something about integrity and decency, and him needing 'a shit, really bad.'

We all ignore him, and the frosted image of his face squashed against the window like kids do - their lips and noses making for a bizarre and ghostly spectacle - and we make small talk. He lingers stuck to the outside of the window for what feels like an eternity but is probably only a few seconds or so. He's like one of those suckers on a toy that hangs to a surface for as long as the spit used as an adhesive keeps sticky enough.

I hear Rob saying that the perfect Guinness should sit just between the harp and the rim of the glass. Everyone has or wants to have some Irish heritage I feel. And since Brex-Shit, an Irish passport to avoid the queues and the stares and the pitying fucking looks and the hidden inner monologue coming from their minds that we're all fucking horrible ignorant thick racist inbreeds who think we're better and more important than anyone else.

On the walls of this pub, I scan the memorabilia. There're framed shirts, football programs, some big names as opponents, some games I was at. Roma, Porto, Zaragoza, European giants who we went toe to toe with. An Adidas shirt used in the 1976 European Cup Winners Cup Quarter Final against Belgian legends, R.S.C. Anderlecht.

I think about mentioning the missing ten years of my life, but everyone seems to be having such a good time talking about the game, the chance of getting in the premier league. And what with Hugh Jackman resuming his sticking his face to the outside of the glass routine whilst shouting 'I'm going to shit my pants here', it really wasn't, I decided, the time, nor the place to go on about my own small worries of how it was I'd lost ten years of my life and now have no memory of my life before it.

"Sorry, everyone for being such a pain in the arse" I shout, unaware that my inner monologue has spilled out of my mouth. The alcohol has gone straight through me. It's my first drinking session for ten years so I'm a little bit lightweight. I wander to the toilets and unzip. I don't want to spoil anything as this will be explained later in proceedings, but all I will say is Ryan has entered the bathroom at the same time.

"Our bladders must be in sync" he remarks.

He then does a comedy double take as I start my piss.

"What the fuck is that" he exclaims "fucking hell."

Ryan is pointing at it like it's a grenade about to blow us up.

"It's like a fucking python, Jesus Christ."

I look down. Sure enough, my cock is insane. It's dangling as far as my knees. In all other respects, it's a cock, with all the usual features you would expect, but it's absolutely massive. Monstrous.
Ryan zips himself up and decides to urinate in one of the cubicles. He takes some time to free himself from his outfit and I suggest it must be tricky being a superhero when you need to go.

He nods, leaving the door open so I can see as I turn from the trough, the stream of his urine as it runs from between his legs into the pan. He tilts his head back as a man sometimes does when urinating.

I'm thinking as I piss. It's something I've possibly always done. There's a feeling of solace, of release. The urinal is a place where everyone is equal, whether you're a movie star, a bin man, a lawyer, a professional footballer, a psychologist, a financial advisor, an optician. You get the message.

So, I'm there, thinking: forget why Wrexham for a moment, why me? Why are you here? Why am I here with you? Is it because you are such good guys, and you visit sick people to make them better or is it because you were in some way to blame for this shit-show? This is all internal. There's no one answering my ramblings.

"Where do you stand on a sit-down urination?" I ask.

"I think it can be a lovely treat" he responds, "and please don't think I'm being a Fancy-Dan, as I'm as down to earth as the next man, but back home, I've had a heated toilet seat fitted, with variable cleansing valves to get to, how do I say it, those hard-to-reach areas. It's just one of the trappings that I couldn't help myself - saw one in Japan when filming Deadpool 7 and had to have it."

There's some graffiti on the wall above my head, a sticker with Chester 125 on it, left by one of their mob no doubt, probably sneaking in during the week. There's also some graffiti by Shrewsbury and Rochdale, and plenty of England flags and a wonderful picture of Prince Andrew with a speech bubble coming out of his mouth saying, 'I'm a Sweaty Bastard'.

As I'm finishing off my pee, the toilet door swings open, and a cockney twang fills the air. A man with long thick hair like velvet, starts running on the spot and then launches into a series of star jumps.
"Alright geezers. Wow, what on earth is that?" he says, pointing in the direction of my crotch.

"I know" adds Ryan, "it's absurd isn't it. "

"Like a third leg" says the long-haired man.

"Anyone ever called you Tripod?" laughs Ryan.

Gary Lineker, new UN Secretary-General, wonderfully silver haired and bearded, enters the bathroom.

"Alright lads, fancy some crisps?"

"Ah, great to see you Big Ears" says Ryan "I see you've been busy, what with the middle east, the cuttlefish wars and of course, all that alien stuff; how's all that going if you're allowed to say?"

Unzipping his fly, the former footballer, famously mild mannered, never yellow carded, from a market trading family, the marketing face of Walkers crisps, has since, as with many public figures with a conscience, entered the murky world of politics to displace those with no conscience who oversaw us all.

"Yes, the alien stuff has been intense. I can't really go into any detail but it's going to be big news. It might even challenge the rise of Wrexham Football Club in the news rankings. You've been number one for long enough" winks the Leicester potato-based product legend.

Gary goes as if he's going to add something but instead appears distracted. He looks down towards my crotch and proclaims: "Jesus, do you need a license for that?"

Ryan is keen to find out more about the alien stuff. He looks at me. I've finished pissing but don't want to miss out on this conversation, so I leave it dangling, looking like I'm still in the act of urination, a cunning ruse.

Gary looks to me and then back at my crotch and then to Ryan. I hope he doesn't notice there's nothing coming out.

"Ok, and this is under the strictest confidence, understood?" says Gary, showing a steely sternness which, you wouldn't expect from the softly spoken, former TV presenter.

"Understood" we respond in unison.

Gary confirms in a somber tone, typically used by newscasters at the end of the bulletin, reporting the passing of some ancient Hollywood type.

"We have been contacted by an alien race; they have contacted us in peace, with a view to exploring a collaboration on various topics: science, culture, technology – that kind of stuff, things that could really enhance the well-being of society", he explains. "Their chief communicator – A.L.F. wants to spend a day integrating into human society to see if there's any compatibility and synergy, and any scope for some form of joint venture."

"Wow, that's truly unreal" says Ryan.

"Out of this world" I add, hoping to prompt a run of puns on the subject. I adore punning. As an aside, I was stunned when one of my heroes Steve Coogan mentioned in an interview that "puns were the lowest form of comedy."

I prefer to regard the pun as something of an art form, a skill only exercisable by the quick witted. I love you Steve, but unless you've been misquoted, can we please urgently reconsider your stance on this.

"Anyway", says Gary, "there's going to be a top-secret guest at the game today. I've not been at liberty to tell you until now but having studied the human condition over the past few millennia, our alien neighbours considered attending a football match was the best way of gauging human behaviour to see if there was any synergy between the two races moving forwards. He's, as you might imagine, heavily disguised as a 'typical football fan' so as not to arouse suspicion. He will be known to you simply as A.L.F."

"Wow, so you're saying there's a real-life alien here today" asks Ryan.

"That's exactly what I'm saying Ryan; he'll be neutral, as you'd expect" adds

Gary, "but between you and me and the goalpost, I hear he's got a soft spot for Wrexham Football Club, and has really engaged in the whole good news, underdog, fairytale bollocks."

We leave the bathroom and return to the pub.

Gary points to a figure in the corner, playing the fruit machine, a holographic image, way more futuristic than I remember. He's striking for his abstract attire: white football shorts and socks without emblem or image, a pair of yellow wellington boots, a black jacket by Stone Island, with one of those goggle masks the hooligan youth wear, like a uniform for a sinister army of violence. He doesn't look like he's from these parts. He certainly wears the label of the proverbial alien very well.

The machine wobbles and lets out a siren. A voice that sounds like Darth Vader shouts "WINNER". On the screen, a button appears with £1000 on it and a direction to press the button to automatically transfer the funds to your account. It's a million miles away from when coins used to come hurtling out all over the floor in the Arcade in Pontins in Prestatyn or on Rhyl Promenade, tourists, clamouring all over it to get their hands on your treasure.

On another table, Michael Sheen and Rob Brydon are arguing about a tourist tax, the Welsh and Scottish Governments are considering charging on English tourists.

Sheen is delivering one of his impassioned speeches, saying "the English are nothing more than thieving leeches who plunder the resources of others. They've done it the world over, for centuries, and it stops right here, right now."

Sheen brings up the topic of dog shit. He mentions he's bringing in tough legislation on dog owners who don't clean up their dog's shite. He's proposing custodial sentences for repeat offenders. The 'it was sloppy so I couldn't pick it up' defence dog owners often put forward just won't wash.

Brydon and Gilbert are nodding in silent agreement. Steve Coogan is saying it's an outrage and is saying this to Rod Gilbert, who's fish punning with Frankie Boyle and Frank Skinner, who says, all this talk is 'shellfish' and 'change your tuna' and Steve Coogan, in his Alan Partridge voice says, this type of comedy is 'soulless' and Rob Brydon retorts with 'you're a ray of sunshine.'

Mike Peters from the Alarm starts singing his hit single 68 Guns replacing the word 'guns' with 'cod.'

Coogan finishes the conversation saying, "there's no porpoise to any of this."

Tom Jones emerges from the shadows and says, "it's not unusual to like fish-punning" and "I bet Paul Mullin is worth a few squid" before heading to the pool table to have a game against Spencer Harris, who excels at pool and table tennis.

The match is a tight affair, with ten minutes of safety play and eventually, Spencer beats Tom in a black-ball game, cutting a tricky black into the left middle pocket. Tom wants a rematch, but Spencer says he wants to take his seat and savour the pre-match atmosphere.

Tom suggests a game of darts to anyone who will listen, but nobody appears interested, apart from Robert Carlyle but Wayne rightly says he's too crazy to be given anything that can double up as a weapon. Tom resorts to playing 'around the clock' on his own. He isn't very good and gives up after missing '1' with twenty-four different attempts.

Bret Easton Ellis is playing Scrabble with Chuck Palahniuk and there's a row about the word 'xi' which Bret has landed on a triple word panel, and which is potentially match winning. Chuck challenges this and there's an argument which Irvine Welsh resolves by consulting the online Scrabble dictionary that allows the word, giving victory to the American Psycho author.

On the TV in the corner of the room, a newscaster reports on sightings of the Yeti in Anglesey. In Scotland, a local landlord believes he saw the Loch

Ness Monster in a pond just outside Arbroath.

In the Atlantic, Derek the Weatherman, in a pre-recorded forecast (as he's also at the game) warns that Storm Brian is heading towards us. Someone mentions the infamous weather forecast by Michael Fish who incorrectly predicted a hurricane wasn't coming our way, before it did, smashing the country to smithereens. Someone said Michael Fish is a pun. Steve Coogan yawns and says, "we really need to FIN-ish this now."

In sport, all cameras are on The Racecourse Ground, with drone images showing beautiful aerial images of the city of Wrexham playing out below.

Outside, renditions of football anthems play out, drifting on the summer breeze 'Yma o Hyd' - the famous song by legend by Dafydd Iwan, about the survival of Welsh culture and language and which translates into 'we are still here, in spite of everyone and everything.'

It's a rousing anthem that's been adopted by Wrexham Football Club and the national side.

Then there's some anti-English chants:

'You're just a small town in Wales' - a reference to the fact that part of Chester's ground straddles and falls within the Welsh border, something Wrexham fans delight in.

'Shit ground, no fans'- a reference to Chester's stadium being unimpressive, and their fan base much smaller than Wrexham's.

We ordered another round of drinks. I ordered some Scampi Fries. Gary Lineker obviously orders some Walker's cheese and onion. Coogan goes for Bacon Fries. Ryan, salt and vinegar McCoy's. Humphrey says you really can't beat the crinkle cut range by Marks & Spencer.

It's a decent shout. My mate Stephen says the Tato range from his native Ireland are amazing and he has them shipped in special. His dad thinks he's gone all posh and can't understand why he left Ireland in the first place. He thinks England is shit and all English are wankers. Stephen explains he lives in Wales and supports Wrexham and that appears to appease him.

My mate Glyn takes a swig of coffee from his flask made by his wife, Sue and decides on ready salted Piper's. Colin goes for a Scotch Egg and pork scratching's, the greedy bastard.

Dr Chris from the TV tells me scampi fries are like eating poison and I'm essentially killing myself right there. Rob is eating low-fat Quavers and is looking evangelical about the whole thing. I tell Dr Chris to go fuck himself and explain, this is what match day is all about, eating shit, getting some pints, and watching the game. He walks off, snacking on some raisins.

There's a thud on the window and one of the doormen, Malcolm, a hard looking Polish man with a Wrexham accent, says Hugh Jackman and his entourage are starting to cause a real problem and he fears there could be trouble outside with the Wrexham Front Line being in the vicinity. For the uninitiated, the Wrexham Front Line is a long-established section of supporters associated with a particular form of fanaticism.

Rob looks to Ryan who turns to Wayne and says "Well, what do you say - shall we let them in?"

Ryan looks towards the window where he can make out the imprint of Wolverine against the glass.

"For fucksake" says Wayne, "he's going to come through the window. We better let the fucker in."

Wayne turns to Malcolm and heads for the door. He goes out, shutting it behind him. After an inaudible conversation he comes back in with Wolverine and his entourage of five men and one woman.

"What you all having?" asks Shelley.

"We better try this Wrexham Lager everyone's getting excited about" says Hugh Jackman.

Shelley obliges and brings over the pints to a table where Wolverine and his group now sit, opposite. On the jukebox, someone has put on Welcome to Wrexham by Declan Swans. The atmosphere is tense.

One of Hugh Jackman's crew, a Scottish actor, Gerard Butler, spits out the beer and in over-exaggerated actor style, gives it: "fuck, that tastes of pish." Ewan McGregor nods his head in agreement. Robert Carlyle, always looking like he's on the brink of kicking off, thinking he's still in a scene in Trainspotting, lobs a pint glass over his head, that Wayne the Landlord luckily catches to avoid any injuries. Leith's finest, Irvine Welsh, wearing a full Hibernian kit, shouts "go for it, Robbie! Smash the place up."

"Have some respect" says Hugh, "it's what the inbreeds drink here, with their six-fingers, the freaks."

Bootlegger, the famous Wrexham blogger and internet sensation, branding face of Wrexham Lager and their Bootlegger Beer, emerges from the shadows of the bar, wearing his trademark dark green helmet. He confronts Jackman. "What are you calling pish?"

Jackman tries to maintain an air of cool, but he and his entourage look like they're shitting themselves. It feels like it's going to kick off, big style.

The man with the long hair is introduced as Joe Wicks. The likeable Essex Boy is by all accounts the current prime minister of the country, a man famous originally for his fitness videos introduced during the pandemic.

"Come on everybody, violence never helped anyone: let's do some burpees; that'll get rid of some of this nervous energy" Joe says.

He starts to do some lunges and then some burpees, leaning down with a wonderful posture. The room all stand and instinctively follow suit. It's like he has some hypnotic power. He makes small talk in between exercises. The tension begins to dissipate; a combination of the endorphins released by the exercise that make you feel good, and his incredibly likeable way, makes for an improved atmosphere.

Joe Wicks is a man you'd like to go for a beer with. Joe Wicks is someone who could dissolve conflict with some star jumps and a burst of running on the spot.

Lineker chirps in with, "Surely lads, if we can sort out the Arab Israeli conflict, the Iceland-Norwegian Cuttlefish dispute, and make inter-galactic relations with an alien race from a faraway solar system, we can stop a little super-hero Marvel sponsored, franchised tiff?"

Ricky Gervais agrees and suggests a game of Rock, Paper, Scissors might be a better way of sorting out the disagreement. Ryan sips his beer and stares at the TV screen. A clip is showing of Donald Trump walking gingerly in a prophetic robot suit along a golf course with Elon Musk, chased by a man in a kilt who's trying to get to Trump (judging by his aggressive demeanour).

An entourage of men in black suits and baseball caps with 'Robot Trump for President' written across them are holding the irate Scotsmen back. Robert Carlyle is screaming towards the TV, saying, "Go on Hamish, smack the fucker."

Wolverine says he's never seen such a hostile atmosphere before, and he was in Washington the day Trump tried to storm the capital. And he's been to some vicious boxing matches in his past.

"Oh, it's intense," I explain "I'm sure there was a stat out there at one point saying that out of all the local derbies in the UK, Wrexham versus Chester had the highest ratio of arrests for public disorder. There's been some terrible violence over the years. I remember there being a load of stabbings at a game in Chester; loads of people went down for that. I remember being at a game when they'd come out and we were sitting just across the corner flag from them. I sat with my head down for the whole game. For your Front Liners and the 125's, it's a very special occasion."

"Yeah, you're lucky we let you in, you fucker" says Ryan, rather unhelpfully. I'm not sure whether the conflict between these characters is fictional, pantomime almost, but it does appear to be authentic, unless they're just exceptional actors.

We let them finish their beers and then Malcolm escorts them off the premises, Ryan giving them a wanker sign as they leave the pub. We have a double Aviation Gin over ice, after our pint, to settle the nerves. We have a game of pool and I beat Ryan in a black ball game. Rob puts Sex on Fire on the juke box, by Kings of Leon.

We thank Wayne and Shelley and make our way back to the ground through a tunnel that now links the pub to the suite in the stadium. It's ingenious and curious, like something out of make-believe, you couldn't make it up.

"It helps avoids the crowds" explains Humphrey "and you can get pints hand delivered" adds Rob, his baseball cap with Wrexham A.F.C. turned back to front making it look like he's from a boy band back in the 1990s.

Back in our seats in the suite in the Jaunty Goat Mold Road Stand, Ryan says in a way, he's relieved he didn't discover football until he bought the club, as he didn't know if he could have coped with the levels of angst and anxiety. I explain that it can be a real mood-sucker but can also provide an antidote to the shit that might be happening in your life.

A 3-2 last minute victory over Darlington might overwhelm the fears that the lump you found last week on your balls, is not terminal cancer, the 1-0 win over Ebbsfleet United might make you feel better despite the death of your Nain, the 2-1 victory over Scunthorpe United might take the edge off the grief caused by Joanne Allen dumping you after a 4-year relationship (bitch). It can overwhelm, distract, bring people together, make you cry with despair and euphoria.

As I gaze over the stadium, I notice the floodlights are different. I explain the feeling I used to have as they come into view, the twinkling of those lights as you snake along the A483 evoking an emotion that a hundred-metre grid of steel, lens, bulb, and cable that shouldn't really happen to a functioning human being.

I've been up close, took arty shots for my Insta as I look up with my iPhone from its base, framed like a sculpture beyond the perfect glass-blue sky, fuddled with cartoon-like, fluffy cumulus clouds that make your heart ache for its beauty. They do look a bit different from what I remember. It's either my memory, or they've installed some big new fuck-off version.

I think it's the moments in time, the past, your own indeterminate history that only you can fathom and dissect and laugh and sob over. The moments you hurtle down the motorway with whatever thoughts and fears and dreads and joys and hope that might be present at that snapshot of time, that freeze framed Polaroid in the memory bank, your own personal vault impenetrable to anyone but you.

Look at me here, I'm getting all nostalgic and melancholic over some fucking floodlights and that's perhaps the entire point I'm trying to make, haphazardly, as a meandering river might twist and turn, fighting its way through the floodplain from mountain to sea.

It's those things. The indescribable layers of object and memory, of minutiae, of detail, of fabric and weather, of dates only you can recall, data, statistics, middle names of players who did jack shit, but who managed to etch themselves into your very own headspace of wasted fact that even if you tried, will be with you until the day you die or you lose your mind or worse still, become a Chester City fan.

The people close to you have got ill, died, dumped you. Life's everyday shit hurtles towards and past you, sometimes taking you out with the force of a decent sized juggernaut or a two footed tackle from Mark Creighton (a player nicknamed the Beast). The one constant during this life cycle is the experience of going to the game, the gridlock, the people you meet at the games, the pre-match pint, the stink of fried onion, the glow of the floodlights setting alight the sky with a thousand rays of hope and joy.

Ryan asks "What's it like to be Welsh?" I say it might be something like being Canadian on one level. Of not being American. It's a bit like that. The first thing you feel you need to explain, especially when you're overseas, is that you're not English, you're Welsh. You then mention Gareth Bale, Tom

Jones, Shirley Bassey. In an extreme circumstance, I've even been known to quote Shaking fucking Stevens.

I want to make it clear that I'm not xenophobic. Christ no. I like to think of myself as diverse in the extreme. But when it came to the location of the birth of my first offspring, enough was enough.

Now, to those of you out there, of a particular persuasion, I completely appreciate this is outside of your control. You didn't ask to be born English. It was somewhat hoisted upon you. After a skirmish in the uterus, you fertilised and fell into the world wherever your mother lay; you had no control over any of this.

But I did have some control over the scenario unfolding before me as clear as the day that dawns. We lived in Chester, just over the border. The antenatal procedures were taking place in the city's hospital from where the inevitable birth, soon to take place, would be processed.

I woke up one morning. It was a glorious spring day. The dawn chorus was chirping with birdsong. The sun was casting shadows across the room. It suddenly dawned on me that my first born was, through no fault of its own, going to be born in England and thereby technically, be English. It could have been the weather, but I came over all flushed and funny feeling. It couldn't be. I had to divert the course of pending history before it was too late.

I then noticed the floor where my loved one was sitting, looked damp, the sun glistening on it. On closer inspection, it was more of a pool than a film of moisture. It was the precursor to birth, the breaking of the waters. Fuck. The baby was coming. Worst still, the English baby was coming, hurtling into this world on the altogether wrong side of the border.

I threw the packed bag into the boot, told Sarah to get her seat belt on, and started the engine. As I rocketed down the A483, unconcerned as to the unmarked police car that always sits on the bridge at the Gresford turnoff, I thought of the anti-Welsh stuff that justified my feelings of anti-Englishness.

The pillaging of Welsh resources.

Inhabitants of Chester being allowed to, after dark, shoot with a crossbow, a Welsh man without penalty (bullshit by the way, it is murder, plain as day).

The town hall clock in Chester having no clock face on the section that looks out over Wales as the English 'wouldn't give the Welsh, the time of day.'

Colonialism.

The Royal Family.

Did I mention the pillaging of Welsh resources?

And so, long story short, I took this journey twice, hurtling faster than a Paul Mullen penalty, from Chester to the Wrexham Maelor Hospital, my two kids, Ianto and Iolo, being born in Wrexham, within the glow of the floodlights of Y Cae Ras, The Racecourse Ground, Wrexham. It was an emotional journey, and well worth the speeding fine.

Rob, Ryan, and Humphrey are suitably impressed by this tale of heritage and loyalty. As an aside, I mention that Ianto didn't have a name for three weeks as we had understood he was going to be a girl and not a boy. So, we had a girl's name, Betsi, but no boy's name. I narrowed the list down, after his birth to Joey, Mickey, Jon Paskin, but she wasn't having it. There are limits to my obsession she perhaps justifiably pointed out.

Ryan says he understands the need to learn about what it is like to be a supporter, a fan. I remind him that the word 'fan' is derived from the word 'fanatic.' He asks me what I think about the Red Passion (RP) Supporters Forum. For the uninitiated, RP is a Wrexham supporters forum to discuss all things relating to the football club, as well as other 'off topic' matters 'general football' issues and other subtopics like 'Wales football.'

I explain, it's a hotbed for debate and as with all forums, includes a wide spectrum of opinion, sometimes and often ending in heated debate. In the darker, unsuccessful days, there evolved a broad two-tier divergence of views, one under the label of 'Happy Clappers,' the other the more negative 'Frothers.'

Arguments between Happy Clappers and Frothers became volatile and often ended in yellow cards and in extreme cases, expulsion for a temporary period by a group of administrators whose job amongst other things was to preside and administrate over any forum fallouts.

There have been some threads that have become the thing of RP Legend. There are some real characters on there. I used to post often. My involvement waned with having kids, running a business, writing; life intervening as it does.

I'd often thought it would be great to have an event where we all met up with a name badge showing who we were. Preconceived perceptions of what someone would look like, be like, sound like, act like, against their cyber voice, their personality, the type of human being you thought they would be like against what they were like in person.

It was, I recall, discussed on the forum. I don't think it ever transpired, which is probably for the best. In hindsight, I think I prefer the mystery. It'd be like coming face to face with the Yeti or the Loch Ness Monster. Sometimes things are best left alone.

If you want to fully embrace yourself in the culture of Wrexham FC, I'd strongly recommend signing up and joining in the discussions. Like all forums, it's a petri dish of different viewpoints, some you might agree with, some with which you might vehemently disagree with. You will probably come across FOG, a poster who, love him or loathe him, is the thing of Red Passion legend.

The Live Match thread is particularly enlightening, the extremes of human emotion in real time action as the game plays out in the background is worthy of viewing. The live match thread is also very useful if you're struggling to listen on the radio or steam the game live.

I explain that whilst it can be brutal, like anything associated with the club, the fanzines, the wonderful podcasts, they, the people who create these things, are the most fanatical of supporters and are the lifeblood of the club.

Regarding supporters, I point out the possible elephant in the corner between those who supported the club for years and those whose interest was sparked by the takeover. It could be classed as The Lifers versus Bandwagonism.

"It's an interesting debate," says the superhero, dressed in what I'm just realising, is effectively a red cat-suit. It's a bold and brave look. The other one, with the difficult to pronounce name, says empathetically, looking down at my feet, that Crocs are a definite no-no. I ask him about Man-Uggs, the question hanging in the air like a thought bubble in a cartoon. They exchange looks and don't answer.

"So, what's the criteria for being classed as a Lifer?" asks Rob, "supporting from at least 2000?" I respond by saying "I'd say there are various layers of fan and that needs to be respected but ultimately all the layers come together to form the mountain of support that we have." It's a corny response but it makes sense.

"I've been watching since the 1970s - does that make me more deserving of success than a newbie?" I ask, half smiling, tongue in cheek but meaning it a bit. Humphrey, who has just re-entered the room, which frankly, is getting too cramped for my liking, especially when one of the documentary crew, the bloke with the big furry stick, hovers over where I'm sitting.

"Clever metaphor" he says, "but I can imagine it can be a bit of a thing amongst supporters." I respond, adding, "perhaps, but they'll always a hardcore but I think overall, most people have just encompassed the change and welcomed it."

I nod and turn to Rob and ask if he ever considered changing his surname to something less confusing to spell and to say. He responds by saying he did it for a while but it's part of his heritage and so, he's learnt to live with it. Rob does a wanker sign behind his back.

We talk about the stress of watching sport, the feeling of elation and despair and the thinness of the line that runs between them as a thread invisible to the human eye, only tangible as a stab in the stomach, a gut-wrenching feeling of nausea when things don't work out, when the result goes the wrong way.

We discuss how a football club in a town like Wrexham is intrinsically embedded in the community. When the football club is doing well, the town does well. The mood of the town on a Monday morning after a weekend defeat is downcast, productivity sluggish, energy levels low. Conversely, after a win, the whole place is buzzing, talking about the game, looking forward to the next.

This is more prevalent in a one club town like Wrexham, and perhaps also, in a working-class, blue-collar area based upon industry like mining or steel working or ship building, where the workers escape from their shift to watch their team with their mates, feeling a deep-rooted connection, a place to be associated with, to be proud of. There's a feeling of camaraderie, a feeling of belonging, identity, of being bonded together by a commonality, something that makes you feel part of a movement, a feeling of intense unity.

We talked about the pyramidal system of promotion and relegation. It doesn't happen in North American sport. It adds to the drama, the implication of victory and defeat, and enhances the anxiety, the finality that comes at the end of every season.

It's a concept they struggle to understand. How success and failure can be so finely balanced, margins often flimsily based upon the outcome of a single game at the end of the season; a missed penalty, a bad refereeing decision, altering the course of history in the blink of an eye. I explain I only experienced three promotions during my time supporting the club, and more relegations that I care to count.

The thing with sport is, I explain, without stating the obvious, there's no control over the result (unless you're in charge of Juventus in the 1990s). There's no script. Those who create films and TV shows know exactly the direction the show is going to take, the context, the tone, its genre, whether it wants to make you laugh, smile, cry, drench yourself in melancholy, or euphoria or fear or joy.

You get the message; the creator is in control. In sport, you can exert as much preparation as you are prepared to put in and attempt to influence the success or otherwise of the result, but ultimately once the referee blows the whistle to start the game, the result is largely out of your control.

I explain that football is in your blood, it's part of your DNA. It's a rite of passage. It passes through generations. You're stuck with it, like a fingerprint. For me, my father took me from Prestatyn with his mates from the dubiously named 69 Club, to the nearest league club, thirty-eight miles down the road. At that time and since, the easy transport links to the northwest of England made supporting the likes of Liverpool and Everton and the Manchester clubs incredibly easy.

He wanted me to support somebody Welsh, and as the only Welsh club in the north of Wales, this was the only option. I was instantly hooked. The stench of cigarettes and cheap lager, fried onion, the stink of regular defeats, helped shape a strange and sometimes paradoxical love affair, something that often seemed to provide more despair than euphoria. But the tattoo had been well and truly metaphorically inked. It was part of me, soaked within my heart and soul.

"I'm glad in a way I didn't get into this when I was younger. It would have taken over my life. I'd never have got round to creating Deadpool" he adds.

"That's where I know you from" I say. "I knew I'd seen you before."

"It could also have been the Armani adverts, the Aviation Gin, the credit cards, the spectacle range, and I could go on" says the other guy.

"It's beautiful torture" continues the Deadpool guy.

"It's a good way of describing it" I say. "I've been analysing it to death for years, ever since I had rational thought. I knew it was deeply irrational how something so on the face of it, inane, a sport, a game, could affect me so deeply, to the core, affect my moods, my outlook, ultimately, how I feel."

A gust of wind throws up a plastic Aldi bag in the sky. They all watch it. It's strange the mesmerising effect a plastic bag, dancing in the wind, can have, regardless of how famous you might be.

"I've watched them for over 50 years. I'd love to know how many wins, defeats, and draws I've watched play out. I'm guessing I've had more disappointment that euphoria" I say.

"Well, hopefully that might change a little" says Rob.

They watch the bag dance into the sky, drifting past a V of geese, migrating somewhere away from here.

"We appreciate this has all been a lot to take in, it's something you really couldn't make up" says Rob.

"It's really up there in terms of scripting, you have to admit, it would be a great story" adds Humphrey. "Anyhow, we'll give you a bit of time and space to process it all."

They head off from their seats to the director's box with their guests, an eclectic mix of celebrities, politicians, and some old friends, as they make their way to the corporate hospitality for some pre-match entertainment.

Presidents Zelenskyy and Gorbachev, Spencer Harris, Joe Wicks, Madonna, Bootlegger, Bryn Law, Tom Jones, Gareth Bale, Fizz from Coronation Street, manager of Premier League, Walsall, Dean Keates, Steve Massey-Ferguson, Derek the Weatherman, Huw from BBC News, Mike Peters, his wife Jules, my mates Glyn, Alan, Stephen, Colin and Jason, all disappear down the steps, enjoying their day out at the hottest ticket in town.

Some players are warming up, dressed in skin-tight super-Lyra, a modern fabric designed to make you slightly less shit than the other team who can't afford such luxuries. It's a strange place, a football stadium, there's something cathedral about it, spiritual almost, and I'm not a religious man.

Beyond the stadium and the floodlights, the cityscape of church, the railway station, the brewery, buildings old and new, beneath the glorious rolling countryside of fields and hills, and I watch the crowd snaking through the grid of familiar surrounding streets: a sea of faces, amongst them, there's Spidermen, Deadpool's and Wolverines, some Hulks and a wayward Zippy from Rainbow, all draped in Stone Island, Armani, threatening to skirmish.

There's the sound of anticipation, an explosion of emotions pent up over decades of decay and deterioration, a collective chorus, of a million joyous voices hanging in the summer sky, a full sun arcing beyond the stadium, above the distant purple hills, the sky taking on a golden shade, the evening drenched in seemingly endless, warm amber sunshine.

Beyond a silence that often preludes a storm, or some otherworldly event, the wind drops, the colour from the day, starts to fade away, and as dusk falls, the sky is a million shades of beautiful, Wrexham red.

You'll know all about the 2020s of course, unless, like me, I'm guessing you haven't been sat on your backside, kept alive by machines feeding you a smoothie of liquidised kale served at room temperature like a fine Beaujolais, through a tube.

You'll have seen all the crazy stuff that's gone on. Each and every one of you has been witness to a truly surreal decade that even the most gifted of screenwriters couldn't have conceived.

There's the fall of a monarchy, Russia and its invasion of Ukraine, the assassination of Donald Trump and Vladimir Putin, the return of Gorbachev, Joe Wicks and Bear Grylls entering politics and becoming prime minister, the demise of the Tories, the imprisonment of politicians, alien collaborations, your fifth-tier football team rising up the leagues.

You could say, with a sense of massive under-statement, it's been a crazy ride; as it says on a mug, I drink my morning coffee from 'Life is after all, an endless series of train-wrecks with only brief, commercial-like breaks of happiness'.

I'll try and tell it as it happened, through the eyes of those who have documented this. The thing is, when you weren't there, you're dependent on the bias and the lens of the people who were around to tell the story. That's life, that's history, it's how stories are painted.

After everything I've been shown, all I've been told, it's been a crazy decade. It's hard to take it all in. Well done if you survived it. So many didn't. Some might say society has come out better, learnt something from the experience, changed their pre-pandemic bullshit ways. For some it's come out worse of course, way out left-field worse. Everyone has their own experience, their own story to tell; this is mine.

Yes, I make no apologies about it; this is unashamedly all about me. Whether you believe what I'm about to tell you is up to you. All I can say is, I don't think I dreamt it, unless I'm still in a coma, laid out on my bed, a ventilator breathing for me, my brain in a constant dream-like state.

If this is a dream, you'd have to say, it's a fucking marvellous one and better than that recurring one I have where everyone but me has turned into hammerhead sharks and then the one where I'm married to Margaret Thatcher and then the one where the living head of Donald Trump in a jar, is hiding out in my cellar.

If all this stuff I've been shown, this match I'm just about to watch isn't a dream, then all I'll say is, crazy shit maybe does happen, and maybe super-heroes do exist. It's corny as hell, but when you look at all the weird stuff that's happened lately, maybe, just maybe, dreams really can come true, the underdog can have its day, the underachiever can become anything it wants.

The thing I'd say is, amidst the death and the masks and the mistakes and the kindness and the heartbreak, there are always stories out there that make you smile, make you believe in the beauty of humanity, the power of dreams and ultimately to perhaps, ask that question; fuck man, are you shitting me - did that really happen?

Day 1, 2030

So, let's jump back a couple of weeks to the moment I woke up in a room with no memory of how I got there. The first thing I do is ask for a can of Um Bongo. Would you believe it? Not orange juice, water, or even a nice strong cup of tea, but Um fucking Bongo. There's just an overwhelming quench for the mixed fruit drink that is difficult to fathom, harder to explain.

If you're below what, thirty, you'll have no idea what this middle-aged coma survivor is babbling on about. If you are over thirty, you're probably thinking, ah, I wonder whatever happened to Um Bongo. You might also be humming to the tune from the advert. You know, 'Um Bongo, Um Bongo, they drink it in the Congo.'

Whether you remember it or not, it's a terrible drink. If indeed, you can call it a drink. It's a hideous concoction of colour additives, sugar, arsenic, you get the picture. Despite knowing all this, it's an urge, an overwhelming irrational need; putting it simply, I'm just so bloody desperate for some Um Bongo.

Anyhow, enough of this Um Bongo talk. I should explain a bit about where I am, provide you with some context, give you a taster, to see if you can be bothered reading on from here. I understand there are plenty of distractions out there what with your Instagram and your Twitter and your Facebook and your TikTok and whatever new crap they've invented over the last decade.

Put simply, the room I've woken in, with no memory of anything before this, is a straightforward affair: oblong shaped, off white, pavement grey. It's trendy, the go to colour-scheme of its day; or it was when I first came here sometime in 2020.

If you had to guess where it was, I'd woken up, you'd say in an institution of some kind: a place for those who've suffered a mental breakdown, a retirement village, a last-minute shit-tip at a Holiday Inn Express on the outskirts of Wrexham.

It's a strange experience and I can write about it, rationally, now things have settled down. They told me, or should I say, she, Dr Paskin told me, to keep a diary. Well two actually: one for my dreams and one for the stuff that goes on in the time I'm awake.

Sophia Paskin, my doctor, my psychiatrist, she's my hero I don't mind admitting. She's the reason I'm still here and without getting too melancholic and philosophical about it all, she's, My Maker. She shows me the way, and is ultimately responsible for trying to fix me, my empty cavernous soul, my awfully messed up head.

And now I'm going to tell you this crazy story of how it is. I sit here now, a survivor of a decade that has gone, slipped away into the plug hole of history, trying to piece together things that might have happened back in 2020, ten short years ago, when everything, well, to put it simply, went totally blank.

Enough of that, we'll explain how it happened a little bit later. Anticipation, it's all about keeping something to look forward to, deferred gratification, they call it. And it's inevitably usually better than the actual event itself if you really think about it.

Anyhow, this is what they call a bit of scene-setting, on creative writing courses, just to give you, the reader, a taster, to let you know a little bit of what's going on, of what's to come. You can then decide whether to carry on with this or to check your socials, post an aerial shot of your morning coffee, check your likes, those beautiful, ridiculous thumbs up; feel the endorphins overfill your needy soul with adoration.

There're so many things to do now, so many distractions, and I can only remember 2020; I'm sure there's a whole shit load of new technology to enhance your lives, a decade on. This, a simple story, might be something old-fashioned now but please go with it, it's good for the brain, it's good for you to concentrate on something for more than five seconds.

There'll be stuff here that you will have lived through, and what I might say, could have you scratching your face and thinking 'what the fuck is this fool going on about? He's been asleep, the lazy bastard, for ten years and now he's here, telling me what it's all about'. Sorry about that but, as I've said, it is my story.

Nurse Kearns enters the fray. Before I go on, I should tell you a little bit about her. She knows loads of stuff that people don't know about, such as, for instance, discontinued fruit drinks, confectionary, Marvel comics, lower league football, Welsh indie bands. She's quirky and unconventional.

In fact, on hearing my constant and no doubt, rather irritating musings about the made from concentrate fruit drink, she, Nurse Kearns, announces, matter of fact like, that the Um Bongo brand has by all account been discontinued.

She's animated by the whole sorry story. The manufacturer, faced with declining numbers, rumours of hyperactivity amongst children, and finally, an advertising campaign that was overtly racist, (the television advert and the branded carton itself, depicted a family with bones through their noses, wearing clothes from tree branches), the manufacturer, decided to call it a day.

Dr Paskin explains my appetite for Um Bongo was from one of my earliest memories. 'Memory Blasts' they call them. It's the brain rebooting, discovering primitive recollections, recovering its factory settings. Our job is to piece them all together again.

She asks me to list the other things in my memory right now: this will be an interesting exercise to see the things you might remember, to evaluate exactly where you are at this moment in time. I blink hard and digest this. I reopen my eyes, the colours beneath my eyelids transcending from dark red to amber, to pale yellow. It's quite a beautiful transformation.

I picture a swarm of starlings, a murmuration they call it, that dance and swerve in endless shadow-patterns. It's a thing of immense beauty, something that grabs your soul. Then, a V of geese migrating through a pale grey dusk sky, their collective sound as they navigate over countries and continents something incredibly humbling. I recall a Paul Mullin shot hitting the top corner of the net. I remember the euphoria and the joy that all these events brought me.

I shift in my seat. I picture some faces, people I might have worked with, walked past, family if I have any, my friends, strangers, actors, a kaleidoscope of these faces turning and twirling in my mind's eye. Then a series of images, clicking over like photographs beneath my eyelids, under my closed vision, the colours passing over in pale shades of yellow and orange.

These are the immediate things that come to mind:

Driving to a meeting, the sky was low and black. The morning had been warm and sunny, the sea shimmering on the reflection of a white sun. As the afternoon slipped into dusk, a mist rolled in from the fields that surrounded each side of the road, the headlights from the car carving out a path through the murky evening. The full beams of another car, coming directly towards me. The mist swirling in my headlights. The awful sound of metal on metal.

Being punched in the face in Scunthorpe in the early 1990s. Watching a football match. Scoring a last-minute penalty. A feeling of elation. Leaving the ground, a group of young men, dressed in parkas, jumping out on me and my mate as we walked to the railway station.

A goldfish called Neil Salathiel which I was looking after for a neighbour.

Rattling a tin of fish-food over the tank, pretending it was a maraca. The lid of the tin spinning off, the fish-food covering the meniscus of the fish tank. The fish racing to the top of the tank. The fish eating itself to death.

A cat being run over by my dad as I rushed to get ready to watch Wrexham play Colchester United. He walks into the garden with a spade and a green refuse bag and buries it.

Looking back, I had two cats growing up. I had a perpetual cold. It was only a few years ago I was diagnosed with severe allergies to cat hair that I realised it was the little shit's fault.

You see, Frisky 1 as he became known, disappeared into thin air somewhere in suburban Prestatyn on an average Saturday morning. I was playing for Prestatyn Wanderers versus Abergele Glans Albion, whilst birds sang, bees hummed in a strip of lavender in a pot by our front door. I didn't know when they visited but they were there early, where the spring sun was rising behind the low hills that surrounded the town.

It was the day of the visit to Sunderland, and I was so upset, I wasn't sure I should go. It felt disrespectful. I went and we won 1-0. I regarded it as a fitting tribute to my cat.

Wind forward two weeks and on the morning of playing Newcastle, my parents return home and declare they've found Frisky 1 at the Abandoned Pets Sanctuary. They brought in a box, one of those things cats and small dogs are carried in and let off the hatch and a tiny cat nervously peered out and ran behind the sofa. I could tell in this fleeting moment; it was not my cat. It was a different size, shape and colour; apart from that, the only thing that was similar between this Imposter and Frisky 1, was the fact they were both cats.

I didn't have the heart to tell my parents. I didn't want to hurt their feelings. They were doing what they thought right to make me feel better. Either that or they hadn't taken notice of the dimensions and detail of Frisky 1 and genuinely thought they had found him.

I nevertheless grew fond of Frisky 2, and he soon became part of the family. I only referred to him as Frisky 2 to myself, not to anyone else. There was no need for any numbering as everyone else thought he was the original.

Wind forwards several years, and Frisky 2 was accidentally knocked over, by my dad as he drove into our drive after I had angrily thrown him out of the house when trying to make myself a cheese and onion toasted sandwich on one of those Breville toasted sandwich makers.

I remember clear as day, my dad walking round the side of the house and returning with a shovel and a black bag and then disappearing to the back garden. I had no idea he had just murdered my cat. It was only a few hours later that they sat me down, after a 2-2 draw at Millwall, that the truth was unveiled.

Do you want the good news or the bad news? The good news is Mick Vinter equalised in injury time. The bad news, I killed your cat.

Sinead O'Connor and a story of a friend in a queue, who, to her considerable chagrin, ordered the last portion of chop suey in a Chinese Take Away in Dublin, him singing to her "Nothing Compares to You" whilst crunching on prawn crackers.

Try the exercise, there may be things that make you smile, others that cause you to wince and shudder, some might make you want to scream out in pain and anger.

The past, when you really sit back and think about it, as I'm doing right now, can often bring with it, a combination of horror and sentimentality; that's what the brain does, it tricks you into thinking things were better than they were.

Then there's the celebrities, the actors, the film stars, the comedians, the singers, the reality TV stars. They die and even the inanest, the most talentless, the most annoying, the least funny, are immediately engulfed in a canonization process that suddenly makes them the most important, worthwhile, talented people to have walked the planet.

There are stabs of memory, such as some shitty celebrity TV nonentity, famous for getting fucked on National TV, which come from nowhere. They come whenever, without warning, without reason. It's the brain re-booting, restoring the factory settings. As I say, 'Memory Blasts.'

This is the language Dr Paskin uses. As I've already said, she's - without being a melodramatic drama queen - My Maker. That is how I think of her. She tells me when to get on, when to get off, when to spin around on this hamster wheel of life.

In these early moments after, let's call it 'Wake-up,' I'm feeling a little like a lab-rat some people are using as some type of social experiment, a reality television show being aired on an obscure channel in Belize or the Lebanon or the Faroe Islands.

Sometimes, I stare into a wall or just into space, that void between objects that is I suppose, just flat air, that we take breath from, see through, hear from, smell through. I imagine you might all be out there, watching my every moment, my every fall, my every doubt, dream, desire, piss, shit, wank, as if I'm in my own little television show, like a really fucked up Big Brother or Truman Show.

I have these moments of melancholy, let's call it, where I find myself staring into this void and I might be thinking of something, a dream I've had, a memory that might or might not have happened. Sometimes, I come out of it naturally, and other times, Dr Paskin, Nurse Kearns, others I'll introduce you to interrupt me, purposefully I think, to snap me out of it and to also ensure I do the day-to-day stuff that needs to be done; the mundane things - going to the bathroom, eating, exercising, stimulation, the day-to-day stuff.

So, as part of this, I'm taken to a shower room with a tiny corridor that links it to the room that I woke up in. There's no window or other door. It's completely self-contained. It's again all white, the shower, the bath, the sink, the concrete floor. There's also a toilet by Armitage Shanks in glorious arctic white, the brochure would say. Something to mention, a minor detail.

I'm doing some more scene-setting here, you'll recognise now, as we get to know one another better.

The point to note at this early stage is there's no mirror here. Not in my room and not here in this bathroom. In fact, everything has a matt (if I were being cynical about it) deliberately non-reflective quality to it.

That's weird right? It's not that I want to stand obsessing over my appearance but after ten years out of the game, it's a natural feeling to want to know what you look like, how you've aged, whether your teeth are yellow, your face eroded as headland might, by the passing of tide and time.

This becomes something of an early obsession, and I find myself looking into the inanest of places: skirting boards, floor tiles, the window, a toothbrush, ah, the shower, which must be reflective – no, everything is matt, someone has put some considerable effort into this.

I turn the water to the hottest and stand. I do a lot of thinking in the shower. Well, that's my instinct, perhaps that is what I used to do. In the condensation created by the hot water, I scribble what I perceive to be my name. It comes out automatically as a squiggle I may have used as a signature. Little did I know, signatures aren't used much anymore. You just touch things or stare into them. This is the norm for you. For me this is all completely new.

The other thing I notice is I write left-handed; another stab of memory, of holding an ink pen, a man, a teacher, bearded, grabbing the pen, and placing it in my right hand as I was creating an ink stain writing with my left hand. If he did that now, he'd be sued for something: hand orientation discrimination?

This information I'm about to divulge could be seen to be puerile, unimportant to the context of the story. I have decided to include it nevertheless as it's what has happened. Life isn't always straightforward. I look down. My torso is flat. I can almost see abdomens. It's an extreme way to get a six-pack but I'll take it. The Coma Diet – think it will catch on?

Beyond this, I cannot believe what I see. I'm not sure what an average size is for this kind of thing but I'm sure this is over-sized. Statistically, it can't be right. There's no easy way of describing this. Put simply, it's like I have a snake coming from between my legs. I have a penis that hangs idly at this point, to my knees. I am incredibly well endowed. I'm not bragging. I'm just telling you as it is. I feel like Ian Rush the legendary Welsh footballer who was rumoured to have '...a cock like a blind blacksmith's thumb.'

As if my day couldn't get any weirder, I notice I am chattering away in a language I don't recognise.

Dr Paskin pulls out a futuristic device strapped to her arm. It's a watch primarily, but it seems to serve a million other functions: the time in Santiago, the population in Borneo, the value of Norwegian Gilts, when the next series of It's Always Sunny in Philadelphia is coming out. You get the message. It does a lot of things.

It has also worked out, that I'm talking away in fluent Icelandic. This series of words and consonants is spilling out and it's not in the medium of English which is, I'm sure, the language that I spoke in before I woke up in this shitstorm. The magic watch thing of Dr Paskin is translating what I am saying, the voice coming out part Dalek, part Jeremy Clarkson, part Rishi Sunak. It's a fucking annoying voice.

Dr Paskin and the nurse look awkwardly at each other, trying like you do, not to focus on the crotch area; like when there's someone with a birthmark on their face, a lazy eye, a facial disfigurement.

We've all been there; you know you should avert your gaze, but you end up just staring deeply into what you shouldn't, a morbid fascination perhaps, rubbernecking, without the car crash and the blood and the skid-marks. I realise I'm standing there naked, and they too appear shocked by the sheer size of it.

So, the day, my first, you'll remember, post coma, is, I'm sure you'll concur, surreal, not the run of the mill. It's a lot to take in, for me, Dr Paskin, for Nurse Kearns, for you, I get that. I'm sorry to land you with this but as people seem to say (annoyingly) a lot now, I notice, 'it is what it is.'

Remember at this stage, I haven't yet been introduced to Rob, Ryan and Humphrey.

There are I suppose, a few other things that I feel I should at this stage of proceedings, bring to your attention:

Not only am I speaking fluent Icelandic, but I can also speak Dutch, Finnish, Flemish, Thai, Korean and a particular dialect of Filipino. If you need me to order you a specific nuanced type of massage, I'm your man.

My general knowledge is exceptional. Trivial Pursuit, that board game with cheese wedges, is something I can win at within half an hour. And this, remember, is playing against intelligent peers in Dr Paskin who excels at all matters orange (sport) and Nurse Kearns who is a dab-hand at literature (brown) and geography (blue).

I might once have been on the TV quiz show, Blockbusters. I might have asked Bob for a 'P.' There is footage, but I can't be sure if what I am shown is in fact me. I've grown, in my short time post-coma, to be slightly sceptical about many things. Without much of a memory, it could be anyone, you could be telling me anything.

These are the other things I remember:

I once played in a testimonial match for footballer, Mickey Thomas (Wrexham versus Stoke City) pretending (and carrying it off) to be an actor, who I bore some resemblance to, from the soap opera Coronation Street. When he later played a paedophile in a TV drama some years later, I recall getting abused once whilst buying groceries in an Aldi supermarket, a woman shouting: "What you going to do with that cucumber, paedophile."

I remember that all polar bears are left-handed. When you next meet one, try handing him a crayon and a piece of paper and see what happens, then run like fuck. Or take the safe option, tweet David Attenborough, and ask him the question.

I'm still getting to grips with certain facets of human existence such as irony, satire and whether it's socially acceptable for men to wear UGGs and to urinate sitting down (I hope the answer to both is affirmative).

I am left-handed although I play certain sports right-handed and some both-handed. I recall playing table tennis once, against someone in a youth club, and playing alternative shots with different hands. He took this as being disrespectful and punched me in the face. I then beat him playing entirely left-handed and then right. So, if you're reading this, who's the loser now?

I placed a bet with Paddy Power, back in 2020, pre coma, that Wrexham F.C. would be in the Premiership in 10 years. At the time, they were in the National League, the fifth tier of English football. The women on the other side of the phone, with a sweet, soft Dublin accent asked me: (1) who Wrexham Football Club were and (2) I didn't know they played football.

I told her we had a proud history. We're the third oldest professional club in the world, played at the oldest international stadium in the world, once played in the second tier of English football, have reached the quarter final of the F.A. Cup, the League Cup, the European Cup Winners' Cup… for fuck-sake, how can you not have heard of us?

She faked interest and clearly didn't give a fuck. But still, after speaking with a supervisor, she laid down the bet, and it was filed away for eternity whilst they pissed themselves laughing over their morning coffee, the Irish pricks.

"I just had this knob-head on from Wales, something about Wrexham F.C. and winning the Premier League."

"I know, who the fuck are they? Can you believe it? Jesus, some people just love throwing their money away."

Wrexham has long been a laughingstock but yeah, who's laughing now, Paddy Power? You bunch of twats.

It's a strange old mix you must admit. There's stuff there that you wouldn't believe. The head trauma I suffered all those years ago can play tricks with the mind says Dr Paskin. It can be difficult to decipher fact from fantasy.

Indeed, there are reports from medical journals from across the world of people waking from comas, their body shapes different, speaking new languages, doing stuff they couldn't do before.

The brain is a complex organ, says Dr Paskin. You've had a serious injury. You need to accept this is going to take time. If you want to make a full recovery, you must be patient. For the first time, I detected some frustration from Dr Paskin. She looks tired. Fatigued. It must be a tough job.

I ask why there aren't any mirrors in the bathroom, in my room, in this entire fucking hell hole. I just want to see a reflection. Is that too much to ask? It's pretty messed up that I haven't seen myself for ten years. I can't even remember what I used to look like. Can you appreciate how strange that must be? I mean, I'm sure it has a name, a label, I'm sure it does. Everything does, right?

It's natural to be inquisitive about your appearance. But it's not the right time she says. You're not the person, from an aesthetic perspective, you thought you would be. Dr Paskin speaks calmly, in a controlled manner, but I sense she's uncomfortable with this subject.

What's that supposed to mean? I ask.

She tells me it's my choice and that I shouldn't feel pressured into anything.

Now I'm really intrigued. There's got to be something catastrophic going on. I don't really remember much about what I used to look like but there aren't any red flags that I was an ugly fuck. I'm sure I always did ok with the women.

I'd say, a 7 or a 7.5 if I made a bit of an effort, fucked about with my hair. I can remember having some relationships with women, pre coma, a vague recollection of relationships.

What's going on? Have I got an elephant trunk for a nose? The vagina of a fruit bat for an ear? An arsehole for a mouth? I touch and rub over these facial features as if to reassure myself and they feel standard enough. It feels ordinary.

'Just give it to me straight!' I scream out to Dr Paskin, 'Am I deformed?' The audio level must be sufficient to alert the security bulldogs who enter the room with all the speed and guile of someone thinking I'm about to do something bad to the good doctor.

"Show me a fucking mirror!" I scream. "Show me a fucking mirror!"

She tells them it's all under control but not before one of these gorillas has my neck under foot with the other giving me the benefit of his toe cap in my sides, a real rib tickler. I tell them I just want to know what I look like. They don't say anything, no facial movements, giving nothing away. They're the poker players of the medical world. I can't tell if I've got a royal flush or two of a kind. I'm fearing the latter.

Nurse Kearns, a clear 9.5 on the Beauty Scale says:

"Looks aren't everything."

I say they're more important than you know. And you don't think about it as you are so beautiful.

A life for a beautiful person provides a far greater opportunity than for an ugly person.

And don't give me 'looks aren't everything'. Looks are if not everything, highly influential as to how your life pans out. Have you ever heard David Beckham speak? It's like he mouth-sexed a can of helium. And you think Ryan Reynolds got this far on a superior acting method?

They exchange looks and suppress smiles, laughter, and I can tell they're suppressing like someone in a lift who just needs to let off some gas, their arse cheeks cramping up with the enormity of the pressure applied to keep this fart from hitting the surface.

I emerge slightly winded but nothing more and the security men mutter their apologies through muscle bound necks and then exit the room, with all the grace and swagger of Liam Gallagher mocking a gorilla.

Dr Paskin gestures for me to sit. I hover, watch through the window a V of geese heading off somewhere. She joins me, pulling up a grey egg chair by Arne Jacobsen or someone pretending to be him.

"It's an awful lot to take in, I get that" says the doctor.

I don't say anything.

"It's going to take some time."

I just stare through the window, yearning for some starlings, craving for something to take me away.

"It will take time" she reiterates.

"Just don't rush it."

"I'm hardly rushing it, lying on my back end for a decade. It's hardly the proactivity of champions. I just want to make some sense of it all."

"But it will all make sense in the end."

I look down at my feet. I'm wearing a green pair of Crocs, those plastic shoes with gaps in them. I'm remembering someone from my pre-coma days calling me a 'Croc Wanker.'

I might have tried to reason with them, to explain the comfortable attributes of this rubber-based footwear. I might have said, they're worn all over the world. To many in the medical community, the hospitality trade, they're the go-to things to put on your feet - versatile, light, water resistant, decent grips.

What is there not to like? Doctors, nurses, chefs, waiters, they love a pair of Crocs. In this segment of memory or nightmare, I can't quite fathom which, I tell Dr Paskin that the people I tell this to have me on the floor, kicking me in the ribs, pulling off my Crocs, one of them, crouching down and taking a shit in them.

'Croc Wanker' they say again as they place the Crocs back on me, the shit, naturally making a squelching sound as the faeces is compressed between plastic and skin.

This is another 'memory blast,' They come as the doctor warned, without warning. They can, like all things in life, be good, bad, pleasant, uncomfortable, fill you with fear, dread or make you feel euphoric.

In this 'blast' the wearing of the Crocs footwear created a negative situation and they're a thing, clearly, of division, like many things in this world, such as, Brexit, whether you should support England in sport, whether you should ever wear Man Ugg's or even listen to Coldplay? We all make decisions. We all get some right and some not so right.

I ask Dr Paskin if she ever wears Crocs. She shakes her head emphatically like it's the worst slight of character I could ever cast upon her.

Nurse Kearns?

She shakes her head with all the expressions of, 'Crocs, yeah right. Do I look like a loser?' as she exits the room, to the outside world, and a Perfect Life. I think about asking their opinion on Man-Uggs but decide against it, reasoning that knowing when to let something go is an attribute, often overlooked.

Dr Paskin tells me to get some sleep and hands me a container containing my meds. I knock them back with some ice cold Tizer and listen to the outside, trees whispering in the night, occasional headlights and taillights throwing out triangles of red, yellow, and white that cast across the room, making shadows and shapes and then move on out of sight.

Somewhere outside, or in the corridor, another room, I can hear a Coldplay song. It sounds fucking good but from somewhere there's a confusion, one part of my brain saying, these guys can compose a beautiful song, a crazily good melody, and lyrics; the other side counters with, yeah but they're so fucking annoying it just throws a shroud and a downer over the entire tune and makes anything they do, a giant no-no. It's a weird sensation.

After waking from this coma, it's been a messed up first day on so many levels. Your concentration span is lower than ever, so it might be useful for us all to recap some of the headlines here.

There's plenty to take in, I get that: my ability to speak several languages, the size of certain aspects of my anatomy, and the dichotomy of so many things; Crocs, Man-Uggs and Coldplay to name but three.

But hey, I'm here to tell the tale. After ten long years of being out of the game, laid out in a coma, I'm grateful for still being alive, I don't want you to forget that. I also want to convey to you the feeling that there's some hope out there, some reason for optimism. I mean, if I can survive a decade long coma and come out of it the other side, then anything can happen, right?

As dusk falls, the sun falls out of sight, I close off my mind, shut down my thoughts, concentrate on the silence, watch the transcending colours of the sky that falls into a thousand shades of black, grey, and yellow, punctuated with silver specks of stars and planets. Amidst the chaos and the darkness of the night, I drift into a deep, chemical induced, dream filled sleep.

Day 2, 2030

An explosion of starlings is the first thing I see, my eyes focusing on an unremarkable oblong window, opposite from where I lie in a half-sleep in this room, I have no recollection of entering. The sky is pink and low and the faint sun that appears has a nuclear, alien complexion to it, as if the landscape is from another galaxy, a million years from here.

I feel detached, a sensation of floating over a series of towns and cities, watching the landscapes evolve as time moves through decades, centuries, millennia, from primitive settlements to a stunning metropolis, the sun glinting off skyscrapers, pixelating holographic billboards flashing over in this futuristic urban existence.

This is my first morning post coma, my first dawn and yeah, it's a joy to be alive is the first thing I should wearily declare. The air tastes thick and heavy, metallic somehow, and it takes a great effort to breathe and swallow, my lungs burning like hell, my arsehole feeling like one of Gwynedd Shipping's finest articulated trucks has been parked up there overnight.

That's the medication and the machines that used to breathe for you says Nurse Kearns from behind her iPad 23, as she makes notes, reading data and statistics, endless information from the machines that click and pulsate around the edge of the bed.

A crack in the ceiling I focus on, imagining a world behind it, Tom and

65

Jerry, the animated cat and mouse you might recall bombing the shit out of each other back in the 1980s when cartoon violence was completely normal, uncensored, and an acceptable part of a child's curriculum. Watching those cartoons, I learnt that sticking an animated grenade up a character's arsehole, would, at worst cause decapitation and at best, really fuck with your hairstyle.

Nurse Kearns does the usual post coma, first full day after-waking-up-after-a-decade-out-of-the-game, routine. Talking inane shit: weather a bit chilly this morning, traffic a nightmare, breakfast looking spectacular - omelette with all the trimmings, and lucky me, I'm going to meet my new gym instructor who's going to assess my physical and mental wellbeing. Aren't I A Lucky Boy?

She places another pillow, inevitably white and grey striped, behind my head, and encourages me to sit up. Naturally, I'm feeling imbalanced, an expanse, milky in texture, slowly clearing from a weary punch-drunk vision, like when you've been smacked on the nose or you've drank a gallon of brandy and smoked a million roll up cigarettes made up of cheap stinking tobacco, showing through the pink-white mist.

Everything feels hazy, detached somehow, other worldly (you get the idea), the lines that separate the walls from the ceiling, a cactus on a side table, the green digits of a clock clicking over, a strip light buzzing for the connection being made and through a window, the outside world, an office block, a low white-grey sky like an unknown Rothko in an obscure, unremarkable gallery.

I'm feeling odd, a stab of terror, of not knowing where I am: my jaw aching, legs heavy like an elephant trunk. 'Should I attempt to stand?' is the first question I ponder, at this stage one of a rhetorical nature so please don't waste the effort answering for me.

Tell me this is a hallucination, right? Tell me this is one of those night terrors? Tell me I'm playing out right now in some reality television concept, my every action aired live on some obscure channel. Tell me something, somebody: this is inhumane, it's a violation of my intergalactic right to understand what the fuck is going on.

The brain is a wonderful organ she might say, stroking over the ridges of
the upper cortex, placing a finger in the groove that leads to the memorial
vortex, a valve that runs down to the white matter, the section where
empathetic feelings are aroused, to show to you that I have empathy, that I
care, and that ultimately, I'm not a fucking psychopath.

She might say this is the bit that isn't working for you right now. This might
be the part she is pointing a pencil into, tickling the upper memorial, saying
there's always a chance of stimulation, a pinch-point, a trigger event.

She might say all this whilst chewing on a spectacle stem, tortoise shell
made to look vintage by Tom Ford or some other fancy-dan designer and it
might match her eye shadow, the tint of mascara, the hair colour by L'Oréal
that covers those grey roots and brittle ends with those beautiful almond
eyes staring deep into my broken soul.

Dr Paskin, sort my head out; you promised me you would make it better,
that you would fix me up, make me function again. She looks at me with a
light in my eyes, like they do in medical dramas, and then Nurse Kearns
does the same. They both smell of beauty, fields covered in sunflowers,
birds tweeting around a pond where lilies inevitably flower.

Dr Paskin calms me with a hush and a rub of my shoulder and then injects
something into my arm. Nurse Kearns holds my hands and mutters
something beautiful about the sky, clouds, the weekend is going to be full
of sunshine. The floor stops spinning. I feel calmer.

To my right, on a wall sits a vast series of plasma televisions like you might
see in the background of a TV news show which I might not have noticed
or mentioned before. The Big TV as I will refer to it is an essential
ingredient in the story. Inside the Big TV, there's a series of smaller screens
all showing different images, constantly changing, evolving.

So, keep this in mind, the Big TV is integral to all of this. It is in fact,
something of a real friend to me, and we all need real friends, someone to

share your shit with, someone to look out for you. The Big TV is hugely symbolic. It's my window to recovery and unknown to me, your window into the very essence of me.

As I feel the effects of whatever shit it is they've just jettisoned into my veins, the overwhelming thirst hits me like a vast wave and the first thing I'm conscious of right now is I'm so thirsty I can't tell you. I just need a can of Lilt from a cold freezer, preferably frosted with icicles like you'd get in an advert back in the eighties, some blonde with a perm and a swimsuit and some leg warmers rubbing it suggestively against their face.

Now I know Um Bongo doesn't exist anymore, and the world's gone fucking crazy but surely to goodness, sweet Mother of Jesus, Lilt is still going right? I asked Nurse Kearns, and she might think I'm kidding with her, but she nods and says it still exists, made inevitably by Coca Cola or Pepsi, and yes, you can have it with ice and that can be arranged.

"Fucking corporations," I say, and she nods.

"Yeah, do they still run the world?" I ask.

"Not so much, the world is changing" she says. "There's a growing trend of accountability, of ethics, of social responsibility. The corporations don't have it all their own way anymore, they're heavily taxed, they can't hide behind offshore tax regimes. It's one of the positives of the 2020s. It's one of the 'wins' from the global pandemic."

She says I should really try and drink more water, move away from carbonated drinks and we recommend you consume at least three litres a day, especially with your history of kidney stones.

"Kidney stones?"

"Yeah, back in 2017, you had a couple removed: too much salt, too little water - pain like pregnancy is how they put it."

She makes to say something, to start a conversation. She does that thing people do when they decide it's best to allow the silence to prevail; a fear of saying the wrong thing, maybe of just not knowing what the right thing is to say.

I'm half-erect. It's not the right time but impulses, knee jerks, they can happen at any time, right? We've all been there. In school, studying Hemingway, the Old Man and the Sea, and the teacher gestures to you, can you hand these papers out for me? Come to the front, write out your thoughts on the blackboard. And there you stand, a boner making a tent out of your pants and your credibility is blitzed in one inadvertent hard-on moment. That's a memory? Something that might have happened.

The worst thing is it's not sexual. They do just happen. It's irrational but you are branded a pervert, instantly. There's no time for consideration. It's black and white. The more you think about it, the harder you get. It's no-win.

She's on pause. She's wants to say something, and the silence and the anticipation is killing me. It's something you can't begin to comprehend. I'm waiting for her to tell me I've done something horrific. You won't believe the scenarios that can swim through your head.

She gestures towards a man who's entered the room. He has absurd eyebrows; the type teenagers pay a week of their minimum wages for - thick slugs of jet-black hair taking up more of the gap between eyes and hairline than nature intended. He also has a beard so thick and heavy looking; I swear he's going to keel over.

"I'm Dr Dai Davies" he says, pre-empting a formal introduction, as if he doesn't believe in them, the concept of the awkward space in time, a shuffle in bodyweight, of holding out your hand, the fear of an overlook, a rejection, preferring instead to take control of the situation. I'm ok with that. He has a heavy accent, booming syllables, soft vowels. He's difficult to understand. A Tom Jones meets man-from-the-Go-Compare-adverts meets Anthony Hopkins combination.

He says: "You've been dreaming, talking in your sleep. Something about

Lilt. You kept asking for it. It's a nice drink, especially ice cold, there's no doubt about that. I'm with you. It's a logical dream. The stuff about the rainbow-coloured sleuth, that's a bit more left field. That'll be the medication."

Another person enters the fray. Heavy blonde hair, like a Nordic rock climber, eyes the shape of almonds, a very round mouth, like she's from a cartoon, an animated feel to her.

"I'm Dr Mills" she says, all understated and heroic. She's going to say other stuff. I want to put a silent gentle finger over her soft lips. I want to shush her like you would a crisp-rustler in a franchised cinema, a lover who's ruining a pivotal moment of love, sex, and adoration, with irrelevant chitter-chatter.

She hands me a tumbler. It has the image of a superhero on its side. A stab of recognition. A film I might have watched. I didn't think I liked superhero stuff – don't know why, but I feel a leaning more towards indie films, depressing melancholic shit with black and white slow-motion seagulls drifting through a grey monochrome sky; idiosyncratic outsiders, sucking on roll up cigarettes, talking about the futility of it all.

I take a deep sip and put it down on a side table made of plastic in a vivid burnt orange. It's a beautiful sensation. A feeling of euphoria. Simple pleasures. The anticipation for the drink is satisfied. Typically, anticipation can be better than the act. I recall that. The act is often an anti-climax, I remember from an etch of memory or understanding from a previous pre-coma time. The brain is a wonderful thing she would say. It has amazing powers of recovery.

She says all the stuff Dr Paskin has said to me. You know, stuff like:

'Don't rush it.'

'Let your brain process what has happened to you.'

'It will come back slowly'.

'It's a wonderful organ, the brain.'

She might place a hand on my shoulder.

She might smile warmly, gently murmuring some words of recovery, something optimistic and joyous.

You beautiful saviour.

She takes a drink. Another sip. Some steam rises, disperses, some coffee-froth clinging to her lips. The superhero image familiar. Not sure if it's a good guy, or a bad-ass cartoon serial killer. Trying to suppress some urges. Trying not to think, over-think. It's harder than it looks. Try it.

'Let's think of today as Day One' she might say.

'Let's take it one day at a time.'

'This is the first day of the rest of your life.'

She sounds like a poster on a wall of a group therapy session for sex or drug addiction, for grief, for coma survivors who can't remember a fucking thing. There's therapy for anything if you want it. A label for any type of feeling or emotion. We like to label. Then people can live as they are expected to live with whatever symptoms have been allocated to their condition.

Dr Paskin gestures towards the Big TV, this dominant feature in the room, this central symbolic figure that plays out in the background, the foreground, an integral component of my new life. She points to the Big TV and then to something she's holding in her elegant fingers.

"Before you go to sleep, I want you to see something. There's some stuff I want you to watch", she says. "I'm going to play a series of images on the Big TV. They'll be a lot of information for you to take in. It might appear overwhelming at first. But please try and keep your focus, your concentration. Some of this happened pre-coma, some during the coma.

There's a lot to take in. Just shout if any of this gets too much."

She hands me a white plastic device, oblong-shaped, the size of a TV control.

"I want you to press this button any time you recognise anything."

Dr Paskin, in the background, says to the Big TV, "Play 2020."

The screen blinks into action, within it a series of ten screens, all filled with different images.

One is filled with images of a human in a bed in a hospital on a ventilator, the medical staff all wearing equipment you'd normally see in a science fiction movie. Some data fills the screen, in an endless loop: 'Seven million dead around the world'. 'Three million with life changing symptoms. 'The education of a generation irrevocably affected'. 'The deepest economic recession ever recorded'.

A series of footage from different news channels across the globe. Apocalyptic scenes with pits being dug out and bodies pushed in by JCBs.

On another, images of football matches, golfers on pristine courses, baseball, tennis, skateboarding. Olympic Games, empty stadiums, children on a podium with absurdly large medals around their tiny necks.

On another screen, more people in masks, walking through city streets, more graves, people grieving, people standing in the street. Ambulances, horrific scenes of hospitals, doctors, nurses, more cityscapes, low empty skies with no sound other than birdsong.

On another, an image of a politician on a podium talking to a nation, talk of lockdown, furlough, more images of hospitals and facemasks and empty streets. This then becomes an image of Munch's The Scream painting, the other screens also transcending to pieces of artwork, a splatter-pattern by Jackson Pollack, an image of a lobster on a phone by Salvador Dali, a shark in a tank filled with thalidomide by Damien Hirst.

Dr Paskin pauses the screen and looks across to me and the pale white sky beyond me. She takes a deep breath. "I know it's uncomfortable viewing" she says. "It's a hard watch I know. But it's something we need to work through if we're going to achieve what we need to achieve".

I don't nod. I don't do anything. I gaze at the concrete slab of sky and imagine an existence far away from here, a feeling that I might have had in a life before this, as if life were always elsewhere.

"Tomorrow we're going to view some things that have happened whilst you've been away", she says, as if I've been away on some paradise island for the past ten years.

Beyond her, the Big TV continues to pixelate from image to image, from screen to screen, artwork, images of mountain ranges, arctic landscapes, a clip from a superhero movie, a TV show, strips of data, weather forecasts, sports results, endless loops of stuff, like there's never going to be an end to any of this.

I stare at the patch of sky through the window and close my eyes just for a second trying to find some solace, some peace amidst the noise and the chaos. When I open them, Dr Paskin is looking into a device and I welcome the silence, the lack of human interaction. From outside, the sky cracks open just for a moment, allowing a slither of silver-white light to enter the room. There's some light rain. The office opposite is silent and dark.

"Get some rest she says, you need to recalibrate, sleep is an important part of the healing process. I'm here to analyse your sleep patterns and your dreams. Your brain needs time to recover, to restore its functions."

She leaves the room. The void her exit creates is filled with the low hum of some machinery, the muffled sounds on the Big TV of a muted television news anchor, who is talking, by all accounts about the death of a famous actor, some forest fire, moving then to a weather forecast, isobars tightening, a storm on its way.

73

It's good that I'm just wanting some silence as there's not much talking going on. It's just me and this internal dialogue and the images playing out on the Big TV. Out of the window, as night falls, a grid of streetlights blaze under the chaos of endless stars, and at the blurred edges of my vision, I imagine a comet, thousands of light years away from here, gently hurtling through an otherwise, empty, star-less sky.

A nurse I've seen passing through the corridor, her lashes saggy, fat and long with mascara, eyebrows that look like someone's lined up some pieces of fudge on her forehead, comes to take some data from one of the machines at the side of my bed.

She half-smiles, not looking up from her iPad, and moves away out of the room. On one of the machines that the nurse was looking into, there's a sticky shadow of glue where a label has been torn off. I imagine a factory somewhere far away on an industrial estate on the edge of an unremarkable town, making these things. Robots and people on production lines. Endless monotony.

There's a noise where everything stops still for a moment. A sound that you're not sure about is just inside your head or whether everyone can hear this. A sound of static, a tone that hangs heavy like the sky's about to fall in and take everything that exists deep within it.

I lay awake. I think about life and death. I think about the people I must have met, family, friends, work colleagues, people in the local shop, coffee house, pub, football club. I wonder if there are people who I care for, who I love, and I reflect on whether there's anyone out there who gives a shit, who loves me, who's thinking right here, right now, about me, considering if I'm ok.

It's something I don't think I've experienced before. It's an empty feeling as if there's nothing inside, just a vacuous void through which flows only time and space. I feel lonely. I feel insignificant. A speck in an endless universe. I contemplate that it's possible there's nobody out there and consider that the reality of life is that you hurtle into this place alone and you fall out of it alone.

Day 3, 2030

The dark, fucked up dreams seem to run endlessly through the night, like a horror sequence in the local multiplex. There are guns, torture, hybrid animal people, deep, hellish water, skyscrapers reflecting fire and body parts thrown out from a red-hot sun. Then there's the city crammed with walking hammerhead sharks. And then Margaret Thatcher. And then the living head of Donald Trump in a jar, hiding out in my cellar. Fucking hell.

I crave a Twix. I asked a porter with a name badge with Jim Steel on it, if he could get me the double whammy of two biscuits covered in caramel and thick Cadbury's chocolate. He says with a stutter that they don't do them anymore. "They don't do Twix anymore. You must be mistaken Jim", I say. He stutters something in response. "The world has gone to shit", is all I can muster.

I remember a woman who used to keep them refrigerated and use them recreationally before consumption with a steaming cup of tea. It makes good sense; I mention to him. A double whammy; a win-win. Poor Jim doesn't have a Scooby Do what I'm going on about and perhaps that's better for everyone.

Jim leaves the room, stuttering something about confectionary. 'A finger of fudge is just enough to give yourself a treat' is what it sounds like he's humming as he makes his exit. They were by Cadbury's I recall, a decent enough chocolate bar. I'd put them in the same bracket as a Milky Way. Tasty, but never big enough.

The people here did warn me to be fair that they'd come at me, at all angles, night, or day, without warning. And they weren't wrong. There're a few other things that come to mind from my history, pre coma, these memory blasts that come hurtling through as a blazing comet might do, through an otherwise desolate universe.

Driving on a stormy night and knocking over a badger, it limping away into the undergrowth. Eating a multi pack of Double Decker's and a two-litre bottle of Irn-Bru whilst sitting drunk in a park. A shark on a beach that was breathing very slowly, the bits around his mouth opening and closing like flaps on a spacecraft. A plane flying into a skyscraper. A UFO over a hill above Gwaenysgor, shining like a planet, Venus, or Jupiter, whizzing through the sky at a speed barely recognisable to the naked eye.

It's a weird combination of stuff, a kaleidoscope of memory blasts, distorted by dreams and time and my comatose brain. Jim Steel returns to the room and takes out some equipment and glances back at me as he leaves the room. Fuck off Jim.

I'm feeling euphoric and I don't know why. Dr Paskin throws me a cheery hello or it's a normal hello and it's just my mood that makes it feel cheery. She's wearing yellow Crocs with flowers dotted around the plastic uppers. I mention that she had said she didn't wear Crocs; so, what's changed?

She looks at me a little like Jim Steel does. She doesn't respond about the Crocs or Twix and instead she tells me, like a headteacher might tell a new class at a school assembly, that I need to focus; I've had some time to settle in and now it's time for some routine. She doesn't go as far as saying I should get a grip but it's what she's getting at. I mention the innovative use of the Twix again, but nobody says anything and instead, Dr Paskin directs, quietly yet with a subtle authority, for the Big TV to 'show the routine.'

On the Big TV, flashing up on the screen, a white background with the following written in a contemporary font, something Scandinavian I'd guess, and what they would use in the credits on a Swedish crime drama starring a middle-aged female detective, a sexy type with iceberg-white hair who drinks too much and shags all the criminals she's supposed to be locking up.

TIMETABLE

Time	Activity
07:00	Wake up
07:30 – 08:30	Gym
08:30	Shower
09:00 – 10:00	Breakfast
10:00 – 11:00	Dream analysis
11:00 – 12:00	Reading time
12:00 – 14:00	Lunch
14:00 – 16:00	Leisure time
16:00 – 18:00	Video session
18:00 – 20:00	Dinner
20:00 – 22:00	Watch TV
22:00	Winddown/mindfulness
22:30	Sleep

"This is the routine; it will help you restore the factory settings" she says.

It's an early start I mention.

"You're getting enough rest so it's fine."

She says it's good that I'm having these memory blasts; they're all part of the process of getting yourself fixed.

They're hard to get your head around I say. They're almost trippy. It's impossible to know which are real and which are not.

She says this is completely normal after what I've been through.

"Now, we need to look at your dreams" she adds.

"Let's start with last night" she says.

"Are you sure?"

Before I start, I have clear thoughts on sharing information about dreams.

Rule 1: You should never talk about your dreams, to friends, to strangers. A dream is only of interest to you. It is a thing of tedium to others. It is incomprehensible, a matter so utterly personal, it should be repeated, to absolutely no one.

Tell this to Dr Paskin.

Ok well you insist.

And so it goes that, I tell her what has happened as I slept. You decide if there is an ounce of truth in this passage.

I handed my dream book (an iPad) to the doctor. It feels less dramatic than a physical book, but I nevertheless feel stripped back, my soul exposed to this woman, who must, beyond her professional obligations, be excited about reading what goes on in my head as I sleep. She looks to the device and back to me, takes a deep sip of coffee and then disappears into a distant gaze, looking away as she reads the summary of my dream.

Here goes:

Last night I was making love to a woman and the only thing I could say she resembled was Margaret Thatcher in her glory years: The Falklands Conflict, The Miners' Strike. A great big fucking beehive as we fucked in her Downing Street office. Then, in comes Donald Trump and the Yeti and they start fighting, old style WWF wrestling on the sofa in the Downing Street lounge.

Margaret's husband comes in wearing a full Argentina away kit complete with full kit wanker socks and boots and a No 10 Maradona on his back and necks a bottle of Bells whiskey whilst whistling what I suspect to be the Argentinian national anthem.

The Yeti gets Trump into a headlock and slams him down, into the fireside rug. Thatcher, now sporting a referee costume, slams her hand down, three times into the rug and proclaims The Yeti as the winner. Donald Trump exits the ring, distraught, saying something about fake news and pressing the nuclear button.

She hands me back the iPad, completely blank and emotionless.

"Good read?" I ask.

She doesn't respond. She's neutral, annoyingly unresponsive.

"Is it what you expected? Does it show you I'm an awful fuck up?"

Externally, I'm visualising myself saying this with a menace, a gnawing dog-like face, passively aggressive, goading the doctor. It's unnecessary, I really get that, but it's something knee-jerked, a defence mechanism from bearing my night-time subliminal soul. She says there's no right or wrong answer. It's just your dreams, whatever they may be. Nobody is trying to trip you up. No one is judging you here.

I feel like an enormous prick. That feeling when you've scolded your child when they've done a minor misdemeanour and the telling off is completely disproportionate. I feel like a massive twat, a daft, horrible wanker.

"I'm sorry Dr Paskin. I'm terribly sorry."

After the dream discussion, I talk for a while in Icelandic. It's about mundane stuff, weather, my breakfast, the victory over England in 1984, John Paskin's moustache, whether Dean Spink was better as a striker or a centre-back, everyday stuff. She smiles. It's rare, but it does happen she assures me. "What? Wales beating England? Or waking up from a coma and speaking an alien language you couldn't speak before?" I ask. She smiles, neutrally. A nurse in the background, doing something with a machine, laughs quietly.

If I were ok with it, one of her colleagues, Dr Fox, would like to interview me formally for a journal she is writing for a PHD.

"Certainly," I reply, in a relatively unknown dialect used by the Sami in Northern Finland and then something in North Korean.

That day, after a gruelling rehabilitation session in the gym, I watched The Bridge series 1 in one sitting, without of course any sub-titles, whilst Dr Fox and Nurse Kearns watch and make occasional notes. The dialogue is in both Swedish and Danish and this enhances the viewing experience and I find myself repeating comments, finding certain stuff hilarious in this alien tongue. I can't deny this, this makes me feel like a right clever bastard.

After this, the sky, pavement-grey, hangs low as a shroud, and chimney stacks poke above the trees and the low buildings, spluttering out ribbons of white smoke.

I dream that night, a series of inter-connected dreams; people I've worked with, drank with, had sex with. Family members, strangers I've walked past in cityscapes, overwhelming glass skyscrapers, airplanes colliding in blood-red skies.

There's a sense of melancholy, a thread of things unfulfilled, walking heavy-legged through childhood streets, though the sky always appears cloudless, pure blue, sand dunes of snow-white sand, a lighthouse, a memory of blissful summer holidays. There's also a football match at Wembley, Brett Ormerod has a chance to win it, and quite spectacularly, misses.

'How much of who we are comes from where we are from?' is the question on a talk show that I watch with Dr Paskin, one of her assistants sat in the corner making notes.

She pauses the TV and asks what I think about the question.

"What I think or what the answer is?" I ask.

"You decide" says Dr Paskin.

I blink, a little bit melodramatically if I'm honest, like I'm on the set of some Woody Allen movie based in Manhattan as I flick through some biographies in a bookstore and muse the meaning of life.

Then I pause, looking into the space outside the window, a view of white sky, a nuclear looking sun, bright white through a section of darker, grey cirrus.

"I think we have a genetic disposition that is then influenced by our surroundings," I say, half smiling, thinking that this is half-bollocks, half obvious and why perhaps do we have to label everything?

We start with a script influenced by our earliest surroundings, I continue, really getting into this, and then take on characteristics based on our perception of life around us, the people we connect with.

It's basic stuff but I'm lapping it up like a right arse-lick and I wonder how much of psychological theory is founded upon over-intelligent types giving phoney answers when being analysed.

She looks away and then towards me, blazing a stare deep into my soul. She too looks through the window and I ponder what it is that she sees. It's all about context. She might notice the starlings beginning to settle on a brittle skeletal looking tree. She might notice the glint of a plane, a vapour trail dispersing in its trail. She might be thinking of the sex she had last night, what she's having for her dinner - a ready meal, a takeaway; something brought to her apartment by a man from Deliver-fucking-Roo (if that's still going).

A lot can change in ten years, even with a chunk of amnesia, there's a sense that a decade can really shift things. You don't notice it day to day. It's like the ageing process - you only notice it when you bump into an old friend after a few years, and you struggle to hide the shock that they're not who they used to be and that they invariably look like a croc of fucked up old dog shit.

Here's a few examples of what feels inherently different from my first few days of post coma-life:

New items on the TV from around 2020 look incredibly old, the cars prehistoric, the fashion weary. The adverts which occasionally flash up on one of the screens of the Big TV are incredible to watch. The evolution of how humans decide to sell the stuff the advertisers try and make us feel is critical to our very existence.

Cars are one example. The first adverts were focused on the technical attributes of the vehicle. Then as you travel through the decades, it's more about image, drone shots of cars travelling through tundra forests, then a close up of a rugged couple, sexy and functional, with two beautiful kids, like this is what having this car will make you.

Now everything is done by voice control. The Big TV can be turned on, over, off at the command of a simple instruction. If I want a flat white, extra hot (a flat white at normal temperature is just too tepid) in a takeaway cup, then I just need to shout. The best one is directing the toilet seat to be heated or cooled by a simple verbal instruction. I've got to say, there are a few things better in life than a sit-down piss on a scorching hot toilet seat. It's truly a thing of bliss.

Floors are vacuumed by square robots with large flashing eyes, which are strangely attractive. Windows cleaned by robot drones that flash green when the pane they are cleaning has been satisfactorily completed. A toilet is now cleaned by a robot specifically designed to understand the nuances of leaving the pan so clean you could eat your dinner off it.

Everyone wears oblong watches that monitor your heart rate, water intake, calorific content, proteins consumed, sleep patterns and most significantly, the number of steps you've made that day, all linked to a data-chip inserted in an upper arm, the data fed to central government with benefits, pensions, tax breaks, all calculated to incentivise and reward and punish and stop people from being overweight and generally unhealthy. It's reminiscent of something I might have worn in the 1980s but without the functionality.

They give me mine today, the chip injected with no pain, the data only ever a button away on the absurdly sized watch, along with endless information; the weather anywhere in the solar system, stock markets in Burkina Faso, how many episodes there have been of It's Always Sunny in Philadelphia, the height of Danny DeVito, the latest football results in Moldova, all gathered through a simple verbal instruction.

Like anything, the system is susceptible to abuse and manipulation. For instance, flapping your arms about in an average length shower can bring you 500 steps. I soon realise, if I do this during my morning shower, in conjunction with my exercise regime, I've earned enough bonus step points to have an extra flapjack with my mid-morning coffee. I cope well with targets and rewards. Some people don't.

Life is much simpler and yet much more complex than I remember it. The virus wiped out millions worldwide. I can see with the data and the statistics that spill out from the Big TV, Governments struggled to deal with it, to keep health systems functioning, businesses from collapsing, society from falling in on itself. It must have been a surreal time. It must have been terrifying on so many different levels, I cannot even imagine.

I feel a memory blast of some of this time. A scratch of fuzzy recollections. I remember the wide-open spaces, people-less streets, no traffic, skies without airplanes crisscrossing with vapour trails like empty veins.

Apart from the death and the suffering and the loneliness of many, I think I recall an enjoyment of this simple existence, the beach where we would run into the wind, searching for crab and razor clam with salt scattered over the wet sand left by the retreating low tide. We might forage for clams and shrimp and kelp and hang seaweed out to dry like shirts bellowing in the storms that the Irish Sea would spit into the headland as a vicious scream.

I recall football matches playing out, snippets of these are showing now on the Big TV. The stadiums are empty. There's a strange dynamic hearing the shouting of the players, the referee, the coaches giving instruction from the sidelines. A decision from Governments was no doubt made, thinking that having some sport to watch on television would be beneficial even in this format without atmosphere or soul.

During such times, you might question what is essential, what are the things you miss? What are the things you will do differently if the pandemic passes over like a storm cloud inevitably does? Will you bounce back into the lifestyle you had before, like the way a sofa eventually recovers from the imprints of the arse-cheeks of a heavy person that has been sat on it?

I say this to Dr Paskin, unprompted. I ask her if she can remember lockdown, the empty skies, the deserted streets? Was there something about it that she loved, she now missed? She doesn't reply of course. She is, thinking only of the double-shifts, the unimaginable strain on her and her colleagues as they juggled with unprecedented demand, resources scarce, the fear of the unknown, surrounded by, drenched in death and despair.

I cannot even begin to imagine what it must have been like. I am a selfish twat. I know that. I am, at least, if nothing else, self-aware.

I feel her presence, her mind set in the history of the pandemic. She's got a disorder if you analyse it enough. We all have if you dare to delve. The things life throws at us. Our propensity to cope is everything. Those who cannot are classified and labelled, forever to be noted as a computer entry as someone who cannot cope with the human condition.

I ignore her presence, putting to one side the complexities of being a human being and watch the sun arc around this featureless, bland, unremarkable room creating shadows, changing the complexion, from dark to light, from light to dark. It's the kind of room you will be born in, will live a life in, grow old in, and gloomy as it sounds, will inevitably die in.

On the Big TV, constantly evolving, flashing, images forever changing; a painting, a shadow of an animal, woodland, silently stalking the prey of something lower in the food chain. Now, a banal, sterile, inoffensive artwork, a replication of a lesser-known fiord scene by Edvard Munch -

evolving now into a snake, an iguana, a crocodile, a rhinoceros, some famous splatter pattern by Jackson Pollock, a block of orange over red by Mark Rothko that lingers for a while and then becomes a news item, an anchor-man, chisel jawed, handsome like a hologram, showing scenes of Ryan Reynolds and Rob McElhenney at a football match for the club they now own, Wrexham F.C.

I then turn to Dr Paskin and notice the features of her face shifting, firstly her eyes falling in on themselves, then her nose, her ears, and finally her mouth just dripping away like you might see in a Salvador Dali painting. There's just an orb left that is her head.

This shifts in tone, colour, to a dusty orange, the colour the sun becomes during dusk before it sets beyond the ocean. I stare at this and say nothing. The orb says nothing back. There's just background noise of traffic, a siren, some birdsong, the sound of Rob McElhenny correcting somebody on the pronunciation of his name.

I don't tell her about this metamorphosis of course, which is happening or maybe something happening internally, some form of psychosis, a series of hallucinations, my own personal lens on the world, and rather opt to keep this to myself, reasoning that sometimes you need to know when to keep yourself silent, retain some power in the relationship, especially when there's a psychiatrist in the room cutting swathes through your thoughts, your movements, dissecting your every fucking word, emotion, thought process, dream, hope and desire.

Internally, I scream, I howl like a dog at a full saucer of a moon. I am the wind, I am an octopus, I am the storm. I take on the shapeshifting image of whatever you want me to be. This I do communicate. I'm not sure if it's of relevance but it's better to be safe. I feel today that everybody is the enemy.

Dr Paskin says that's enough for today, and my inner dialogue is telling me I'm fucked, deranged, destined for a life of institutional routine, a rattling pill box, a spaced-out zombie in a padded room where I'll watch these things that don't really exist, play out in my own internal hell.

I don't hear anything she says. She's just a mouth moving slowly, as if a film has been slowed down and the audio is just a long-drawn-out range of slow vowels and absurd consonants. Just an empty mouth telling me the way it is.

She says I want you to watch this, there's a summary of what's happened, like Match of The Day for the decade you slept through. It's going to be pretty fucked up, so we'll take it slow: do a year each day to start off with.

I continue to watch her as she speaks, my perception of her features fracturing, as if she's pixelated somehow as a bank robber or a shooter on a TV crime show. She changes form and I'm watching this transformation with a feeling of anticipation and trepidation which I perceive to be perhaps the same emotion. She changes slowly, I don't want you to think it's something that happens in seconds. It doesn't. It happens over a series of hours.

The initial change is the most dramatic, like everything I suppose; that initial natural resistance to change, the instinct to retain the status quo, the norm, the comfortable now. This initial shift in appearance is that she takes on the form of an amoebae like state. It's transparent and jelly-like, completely see through, without colour. It's an absurd yet beautiful way to see someone and if the opportunity ever presents itself, please try it, indulge in it, it's good to try out new stuff.

She then progresses to a flow of hot rock, molten magma, which is simply mesmerising and one of the most beautiful things I have ever witnessed. Then she takes on the appearance of a ribbon of translucent plankton that sometimes lights up the silver waves at low tide under an enormous white moon.

It's something of a spiritual experience watching this, I feel a wave of joyous love washing through me. It then reverses and within a minute, she restores her human appearance, and the metamorphosis is complete.

Oblivious to this incredible phenomenon, she talks to the Big TV and the credits roll and the voice of a famous narrator fills the airwaves. She tells me to settle in my chair, to make myself comfortable. I sip at a cup of tea served in an orange mug. We exchanged a stare. She attempts an awkward half-smile that hovers in the air like the fluff off a dandelion.

'Play 2021' directs Dr Paskin:

I shuffle awkwardly in my seat. I'm fearful, I admit it, terrified as to what I am going to see, what has happened during the 10 years I've been in a coma.

2021

The voice over actor starts quietly, slowly, an unnerving authority and confidence making his consonants sound sharp and knowing, his vowels soft and brimming with understanding and empathy. The screens of the Big TV are all combined as one vast screen that fills the wall opposite from where I and Dr Paskin sit.

There's an image of a vast patch of earth, tinted orange, a desert complexion to the landscape, a series of JCBs, the camera panning out, a hundred or so in a line, digging through the earth, on the edge of the enormous holes created by the diggers, people in protective suits from a sci-fi movie, place body bags into the holes. The image plays out in complete silence, just the faint distant rumble of the machines, some gentle birdsong, the air gliding over the microphone.

Then some riots in Washington D.C., some symbolic attack on the seat of American power. Former reality television star Donald Trump behind the failed attempt at a coup, a revolution, whatever you like to call it.

The narrator then begins to talk, the image shifting to an urban scene of a crowd of people in central London. After a year of lockdowns and social restrictions, never witnessed before, the world opens again. It's a frightening prospect for some who have got used to a quieter life but for the majority across cities, towns, villages, masses of people come out of hibernation like a swarm of jelly-ants returning to their shit-dumps, throwing crazy, mass parties, the streets rammed with people. Society is letting off some steam.

The NHS confirms Covid infections are still high, but deaths are lower due to the roll out of an unprecedented vaccination program. The opening up and lifting of restrictions, coincides with national sporting events, Wimbledon, the Euros 2020, postponed due to the pandemic and staged instead in 2021 over multiple countries, although most games, are held, for some reason, at Wembley, London.

England advanced uncharacteristically to the final of the tournament. The country goes football mad. The Baddiel and Skinner song It's Coming Home, one of the more decent football anthems over the years, is played over and over by the media and through English streets throughout the summer.

Debates as to whether other nation states in Great Britain should be supporting England rage on social media, some saying we should support any home nation, others in Scotland and Wales, saying over their dead bodies.

England lost in the final on penalties and the optimism and national fever is tempered by ugly scenes of violence before and after the final and then some bizarre social media attacks on three England players who missed the all-important penalties. The divide in England and the wider landscape of Great Britain is highlighted again, just as it was with the Brexit vote, five years before.

Two Hollywood A-Listers are announced as the new owners of the third oldest club in the world, down on their heels, fifth tier, Wrexham F.C. Ryan Reynolds of Deadpool fame, and Armani model no less as well as numerous other high profile movie credits (ignoring Green Lantern), together with collaborator, Rob McElhenny, most famous for long running comedy sitcom It's Always Sunny In Philadelphia, are the surprise bidders for the club from North Wales, who have, like the town they represent, had a distinctly bad time of it, with unscrupulous owners, and more latterly, a noble, yet promotion-less time, under fan ownership.

The international media picks up the story which is reported all over the world. In a time where things have been pretty shit, it's a big, unexpected, good news story.

The hospitality trade helps keep the employment rate up as pubs and restaurants open at a rate never seen in history. Breweries simply can't keep up with demand. People just want to get out again. Wrexham Lager's Bootlegger beer has become one of the best-selling beers across the globe, with YouTube Sensation Wrexham F.C. Superfan, Bootlegger, being the face of the brand. A Wrexham branded gin is also launched by its new owners and immediately becomes an international bestseller.

Dr Paskin pauses the Big TV, inevitably with a verbal direction. "Pause" she says, masterfully.

She asks me if I remember anything about Wrexham F.C. I reply that I think I'm not English, yes, I have a feeling in my stomach that I'm not English. I mention I recognise the club badge. I remember Paul Mullin.

She asks me if I remember Rotherham 1978, Notts Forest 1982, Northampton 1993 (Cobblers), West Ham 1997, Middlesborough 1999, Boston 2003, cup games against Man United, Porto, Real Zaragoza, Roma, that game against Arsenal.

I remember some things about Wrexham F.C. I remember the badge and the shirt. Images of the games mentioned above play out on various screens. I feel euphoria as the goals smash into the net. I recall some of the players, Mickey Thomas, Joey Jones, Bobby Shinton, Steve Fox, John Paskin, Ollie Kearns, Jim Steel, Phil Hardy, Gary Bennett, Martyn Chalk, I remember these games. I was at these games. All these memory blasts hurtle down like dominos as I watch these images play out.

Dr Paskin asks if I'm ok. I take a drink from the orange mug. She directs the Big TV to continue its summary of 2021.

The stock market surges and people spend the monies they have saved during the Pandemic. Joe Wicks announces that he wants to go into

Politics. Staycation holidays are at an all-time high with most people staying within the UK as they can't be bothered by the hassle of going abroad.

Memories of COVID-19 are slowly starting to fade as society remembers what it was like before the world closed.

Donald Trump is photographed having dinner with Russian supermodel, XXXXXXX XXXXXXXXXXXX (name retracted for legal reasons). His former wife XXXXXXX XXXXXXXX moves back to Slovenia to, it is rumoured, no kidding, to run a goat farm. An assassination attempt kills one of his bodyguards, but he escapes with the amputation of his dominant, right hand.

The football season successfully finishes without any further Covid-related breaks. Wrexham drew a game they had to win, predictably playing a dour, lethargic, fearful formation which brings the guillotine down to yet another mediocre season and the reign of Dean Keates.

The clubs' new owners are moving to bring in a new regime that immediately has an aroma of professionalism and an authenticity that they want not only to succeed but in a sustainable and logical way. Phil Parkinson, an experienced manager with multiple promotions behind him, has been appointed as new team manager.

New clubs' sponsors, international titans, TikTok, an entertainment platform primarily targeted at the millennial generation, are unveiled, alongside travel giants, Expedia, with long time local based sponsors Ifor Williams Trailers still retaining their position as local sponsor.

The new owners display humour and loyalty in a YouTube video that displays the products of Ifor Williams. It's a production of genius. They are quickly cementing themselves into the fabric of the football club and the surrounding community in which the club is so embedded.

Nestle brings out a six finger Kit Kat. To Joe Wicks, this is perfect fodder for his political marketing machine, images on Instagram of overweight people smashing the six chocolate fingers often in one greedy sitting.

'Have sex, not six fingers' is his strapline.

Joe announces a new range of Tupperware, called 'Joe Wicks Tupperware.'

Nestle brings an action against him for defamation. A liberal metropolitan transgender judge from East London rejects the claim, citing the defence of truth and public interest.

Joe, standing on the steps of a London court, does a HIIT session as the press await the verdict, the judge joins him for a 20-minute session, finished off with a 60 second plank followed by some post work out warm down after the verdict is announced. The judge tweets #superplank @joewicks with a photo of him, Joe, and the jurors all planking outside the court.

Nestle's lawyer announces to the members of the press, who have amassed at the base of the court steps, some sweating and checking their heart rate on their watches, that their client won't be appealing and will be discontinuing the new six finger version of the Kit Kat and will indeed be reducing sugar content by 50 per cent and will source their cocoa only from certified suppliers.

Joe Wicks versus Nestle will long be heralded in the British legal history as being a real landmark case in Britain getting healthier.

Jason Bateman of, amongst other things, Arrested Development and Ozark fame, is seen jogging in a Wrexham F.C. training top in the new series of Ozark.

Footage emerges of Prince Andrew nightclubbing and dad-dancing in various New York Nightclubs with several women who claim to have been groomed by predatory sex offender, Jeffrey Epstein. Boris Johnson refuses a formal request for the controversial Prince to be extradited.

The Queen, opening a new lingerie department at Harrods, refuses to comment apart from stating: "Andrew is a good boy. Ok, he went through a bit of a randy patch after Sarah, but he'd never go off intentionally with a young girl, although (she adds, looking pensively towards a photograph of her son on a nearby mantelpiece), they can make themselves look so much older now with the right make up, and filtering."

Dr Paskin signals to the Big TV to turn it off. She asks me if I'm ok. She offers me a drink, a snack, and a Double Decker. I decline, just not feeling right here, right now, the urge for that sublime chocolate and nougat combination. We share a can of Vimto and a Lion Bar and sit quietly as I process what I've seen.

It's been a crazy decade she says. There's some other stuff from the past that we want to show you. This might trigger some further memory blasts.

She tells the Big TV to play 'Video Memory.'

The first thing that appears on a screen is a beach scene. On the face of it, an unremarkable clip of grainy handheld footage of a strip of sand, some dunes, some skinny trees beyond with pinecones and marram grass swaying on a breeze. It feels serene, warm, and sunny, the sky low and blue, some fluffy white clouds dancing above the horizon.

A toddler appears, stumbling awkwardly on the edge of where the tide hits the sand. The audio picks up some seagull noise, the lapping of the water, the child squealing. There's a dog and a frisbee and a low sun throwing out spots of spectrum onto the screen, giving it the complexion of an award-winning indie film, starring Greta Gerwig or Jennifer Aniston.

Dr Paskin, in my peripheral vision is making notes whilst watching me watching the Big TV. I'm not letting on that I know she's watching me, and I try to watch as if I don't know someone's watching me. It's trickier than it looks.

I soon become immersed in the footage that's playing out. A man, ink black hair, comes into view, kicking an orange football, one of those leather balls that existed in the 1970s. He kicks it towards the toddler who stumbles over it, pushing the ball along as he walks across the sand.

Some adult noise, cheering, the toddler held aloft as a trophy, the man and a woman, blonde hair in a sharp bob, the woman taking a photo of the scene, the person filming this on a handheld camera, losing focus for a moment, a wonky view of sand, flip flop, sea, and sky.

The movie maker regains some control, focusing on some kite fluttering above the dunes. The kite is green and yellow and vivid against the pale sky. It appears nothing spectacular, rhombus shaped, like a typical kite, but when the winds spin it in a different direction, it takes on the form of a frog, Kermit perhaps from The Muppet Show. It's only when five minutes later a pink pig kite comes in from twenty, thirty yards away, which is clearly Miss Piggy that this clarifies our earlier suspicion that the green and yellow effort is indeed Kermit the Frog.

The puppeteer is out of range of the camera and the sight of these kites beyond a pale white sky is something quite artful, melancholic, if you had to find an adjective for it. The camera spins about and the toddler is being swung between the man and the woman as they walk along the frothy surf.

Beyond them a cargo-ship, then a tanker and a ferry, queueing across the bay, the sound of a buoy rings out, steam rising from chimney stacks on a headland, low, unremarkable industrial buildings, a suspension bridge, an airplane drifting across the sky.

All these things that we might not notice until someone points them out to us, on a television screen, a photograph, a clip that stimulates a memory, an emotion, the feeling that you are indeed, no longer dead to the world; that you are indeed, very much alive.

The scene is either me as a child or my own child. I'm guessing by the dated status of the footage that it's the former and that the main protagonist is me, as a toddler, with the peripheral characters being my parents. If so, are they still alive?

Dr Paskin pauses the footage and asks me to articulate the emotion the video has evoked.

"I feel melancholic" is all I can muster. "I feel happy and sad at the same time. I feel exhausted" I add.

"I'll move onto something less personal, more generic."

Dr Paskin directs the Big TV to show footage of a man she describes as a former President of the United States. The BBC newscaster tells of an assassination attempt. Do you remember him? asks Dr Paskin.

I close my eyes, which is something I've noticed I'm doing when trying to recall events pre-coma. Sometimes when I squeeze hard, my eyeballs feel bruised when I open them. I remember Donald Trump as a reality TV presenter I say, recalling vaguely, some television show.

Anything else?

I close my eyes again, my eyeballs feeling like they might pop and explode in a gooey juice show.

Shit hair, really fucking premier league shit hair. Comb over. Weird colour. Yellow, no orange, eyes closing tighter.

Anything else?

Nurse Kearns is suppressing laughter, like you might do in a school assembly when it's announced that Brian Smith from Year 3 has died of a brain tumour.

I close my eyes and put my fingers to my temples like I'm some clairvoyant Jedi warrior trying to fathom the mysteries of the universe and work out when Evil is going to strike next.

He went on to be president (Donald Trump) not Brian Smith.

Yes, that's right says Dr Paskin. That's right.

She and Nurse Kearns share a quarter-smile.

He was awful. Truly awful. I say, eyes still closed.

Dr Paskin says he divided a nation and created debate that's for sure. She's a diplomat, she's Switzerland, she's a beautiful inoffensive glacier. Someone put a bomb in his toilet in Trump Towers. Went off as he took a dump. Found his hairpiece stuck to the ceiling. There's been assassination attempts every year or so, as you'll see, he's not the most popular man on the planet.

She turns off the TV and outside, the sky is pink and flat frisbees of cloud dance across the sky on a gentle breeze. I have an overwhelming urge for a Marathon. I ask if I could have one with a mug of piping hot, extraordinarily strong tea (the only way to drink it). Dr Paskin laughs. I feel patronised, like asking for a snack of chocolate coated nougat and peanut is the most ridiculous request in the history of the civilised world.

"They don't exist" she says.

Well, that's not actually true, interjects Nurse Kearns. They do exist format wise, but they underwent a complete rebrand some time ago.

"So it is essentially in taste, still a Marathon?" I ask.

"Yes, I suppose it is" Nurse Kearns went on.

"But they've just changed the packaging and the name?"

"Well, the packaging, the design, the brand is the same, but for the name change."

"Why would you want to change that" I ask.

"It was to do with the American marketplace. They thought Snickers would appeal. And Mr. T from the A Team driving around in a tank, promoting that it takes nuts to eat a Snickers."

"Fucking Americans" I say.

Dr Paskin smiles.

Nurse Kearns says you can't tar them all with the same brush.

"Maybe not, but let's be honest, they have more than their average lot of fuckwits," says Dr Paskin.

"The same fuckwits who thought voting for Donald Trump to be president, would be a swell idea," I say, adding the word swell in an exaggerated American accent.

Nurse Kearns says we have our fair share - look at Brexit she says.

Fucking Brexit, I can remember that, dominated the country for what seemed like forever.

Democracy, eh?

Referendums are dangerous.

Democracy can be dangerous.

Dr Paskin places the buzzer on the side table.

"Right, here's some more footage" she says.

She tells the Big TV to 'Play.'

See you if you remember any of this:

Football Match: Wrexham V Boston United: 2007.

She directs the Big TV to play highlights of the match and asks me for any memories that they trigger. Wrexham are playing the footballing giants Boston United. It is the last game of the season and whoever loses falls out of the footballing pyramid and slips into the abyss of non-league football.

Since their birth in 1864, Wrexham have always plied their trade in the English Football League. The significance of this game is massive. It is, without exaggeration, the biggest game in the history of Wrexham Football Club.

The Racecourse Ground is absolutely crammed. There's a party atmosphere, and the weather is unseasonably warm and sunny. People are dressed in red wigs. The crowd has been swelled by those who don't ordinarily attend but who have an affinity for the club and want it to succeed, and certainly don't want to see it falling out of the league pyramid. It would be catastrophic.

As kick off approaches, the carnival atmosphere shifts to a nervousness which seems to permeate across the fabric of the stadium, through the blades of grass on the pitch and into the very bodies and minds of the players themselves. How players react to big occasions like this dictate the success of their careers more than how technically good they are at football.

Wrexham started off incredibly slow and within minutes the unthinkable has happened; they are 1-0 down. Non-league football looms large. I can feel the ache in my stomach. I press the buzzer.

I recall infamous footage of Bryn Law, the celebrity Sky journalist who typically covers high level Premiership football matches for the television channel but today has been allowed to watch his own club in a broadcasting moment which will end up becoming legend in Wrexham folklore.

The Sky Sports legendary anchor-man Jeff Stelling hands over from the studio to a stricken looking Bryn Law as he reports to the nation that Wrexham are 1-0 down to Boston and they are only 60 minutes away from slipping through the trapdoor into the void that is non-league football for the first time in their history.

Halftime comes and goes in silence and not even a cup of the worst coffee known to humankind can lift the spirits of the home crowd. The conversations with those sitting around you are muted. People are stunned, unable to fathom the implication of defeat.

There are grown men with tears in their eyes. A man locks himself in the toilet cubicle as he can't face the second half. He'd prefer to not face the disaster that is playing out. It's that car crash in slow-motion, the horror film watched from behind a sofa.

The second half begins, and an energy rises through the stadium, the pitch, the players. They've risen to the occasion. Wrexham turned around the deficit and won 3-1 as the Racecourse Ground erupts with a relief that the unimaginable was not going to happen, at least, not on that day.

I press the buzzer and with an air of enthusiasm that matched with the memory, I explain I can remember all of this.

Dr Paskin notes all this down in her iPad. "Very good" she says. "Any other memories? Tell me if you can remember anything at all."

"I'm not English" I say.

She then directs the Big TV to watch highlights of a game between Stoke City and Wrexham:

Mark Carrington dives into the Stoke area and smashes a header past the goalkeeper. I remember this and press my buzzer. We're in the prawn sandwich seats and go ecstatic. A bunch of locals drenched in Stone Island try and get to us. If it weren't for some stoic and decent stewards, we'd have been smashed to smithereens.

The Premier League outfit, as they were then, came back in the last ten minutes or so to win 3-1. The only redeeming feature is that it kept the locals happy and probably saved us from a pounding. Instead, they clapped us out of our seats, the wankers.

Then, the Big TV flashes over to the image of Manchester United V Wrexham away at Old Trafford. I press my buzzer. I remember this. Kieran Durkin, God rest his soul, scores to put us into a lead at the iconic Stretford End. We lost 5-2 but that moment where the reality of the situation seemed to come across the length of Old Trafford to where we were amassed,

7,000 of us, behind the opposite goal as a giant wave for a moment, will live on forever. It was like time was suspended, a bullet in a Marvel movie flying in slow-motion towards its target.

An image now of Wales versus Spain played at The Racecourse Ground, Wrexham. I press the buzzer. I remember this I said. A footballer, eighties style haircut, scissor kicking towards a sloping stand overflowing with red and white. The ball hits the net. The crowd erupts. I remember this; Wales 3 Spain 0. Mark Hughes.

I press the fucking buzzer.

Dr Paskin tells me I'm doing incredibly and if I've still got the energy, I'm encouraged to write any memories down. This is what comes spilling out like a fierce wave, crashing onto a long and vast beach during a violent storm:

My dad's mate was the linesman and the linesman fucked us over.

You'd need to double check the detail but it's around the 1981-82 mark and we're driving to the game in a Renault or a Citroen. I know it was French as the bloke driving it was particularly proud of the issue, like he was exotic driving around in something that wasn't Ford or Toyota which is what made up most cars in my hometown of Prestatyn.

The weird thing is, this man who might have been round our place a couple of times for a dinner party with his wife, a woman who spoke poshly with an accent my mother was convinced was contrived for such events.

I declined to interject that she (my mother), also seemed to speak the same way, like there's some expectation, something that comes over people at these events, where they feel the need to cook food they'd normally never dream of cooking, using equipment, extra plates, endless cutlery, a Hostess Trolley to wheel the weird food into the dining room (and note that the dining room was in fact in everyday life, a section of the kitchen where we used to eat together, as a family), with just a stubby oblong of a television set in the corner on a Welsh dresser, then later in the decade, on a bracket no less.

Anyhow, I'm digressing. This man, an occasional visitor, drives us through the landscape of North Wales, a task that then took forever, as this was before the days of the EU funded A55 Expressway. He'd been kind enough to offer us a lift from Prestatyn to the Racecourse Ground, Wrexham, where he is today officiating as a linesman.

Eventually we arrived in the official car park to a designated space, kept free by a couple of strategically placed traffic cones painted red and white with the word OFFICIALS carefully stenciled over one of the white sections of the plastic cones that were otherwise used as hats by pissed up students at the time.

We were allowed into the entrance reserved for players and officials and I, an 8-year-old, felt very fucking important indeed. I see the manager and players knocking around in tracksuits with the Wrexham emblem and whoever they might have been sponsored by back then.

Joey Jones as club captain welcomes me and my dad and his mate, the linesman. He picks me up and welcomes me to the rest of the players, the coaches, the management staff. He hands me to Dai Davies, the goalkeeper and says 'don't drop him Dai' which creates some hilarity amongst the group. For those of you who don't know, Dai was a wonderful goalkeeper who also played for Everton and Wales and was sometimes, with fondness, referred to as 'Dai the Drop.'

We leave for the main stand and take our seats in what would now be the equivalent of corporate hospitality. This was before the days of prawn sandwiches and the elaborate hospitality now available at football stadiums. But it was exciting. I'd just met my idols, those I so desperately wanted to emulate when I grew up.

I watched us go into a one goal lead, and then concede an equaliser. The game was petering out into a 1-1 draw when suddenly, in the corner of my eye, my dad's buddy is waving his yellow and red chequered flag as if his life depended on it. The referee, on witnessing this rare event, waddles over (referees weren't the lean athletes they are now) consults with him and awards a free kick on the edge of the area.

The Bristol Rovers player taps it to another (indirect free kick for handling the ball out of the area whilst kicking it) and he smacks it into the back of the net. Despite this being 50 years ago I remember the lad who scored and his absurd blond mullet and him celebrating in front of the couple of hundred away fans who celebrated like they'd won the Euro Millions.

The home supporters were naturally disappointed and at the final whistle, I recall the linesman walking off the pitch and down the tunnel from where he and the players had originally entered the fray. He was called things I'd never heard people called before and a hostility that to this day is particular to the culture of football. Its origins are no doubt built from a passion and a desire for victory but there's an edge which is a remnant of the human psyche from the early origins of humankind. It's an ugly thing to witness at times.

Football does that to you. Inane memories stick with you when other everyday stuff slips through your hands. It's nerdy. Like collecting Marvel comics, stamps, old vinyl but without the physical product to hold and touch, apart from if you buy the programme for each game and keep them safe. I bet I have a hoard of old programmes. I'll have to dig them out.

The one from the Bristol Rovers game was signed by all the players and the officials. Sentimental objects all carrying an array of emotions, from that day in history. You might remember who you travelled with, the weather, where you went for a pint, the girlfriend who had just dumped you because she knew she was always going to be less important to you than your football club.

I recall the poplars, a row of them beyond the main stand swaying in a warm breeze. They were part of a wider vista, some low hills, which changed colour depending on the season, the weather, some buildings, roads, playing fields, pavements with people passing through, going about their lives. That view, those poplars, they always felt more than a row of a dozen or so trees. It sounds absurd, but I felt a connection with them. They were a constant in an ever-changing world.

Back to the Bristol Rovers game, after the game, in the car park, I recall someone had added a cock and balls to the bonnet of the linesman's car. At the time, at the age of eight, whilst I knew what the symbol depicted, in this context, it was confusing. I didn't understand this was a mark of derision, of dissatisfaction. The passion of a hard-core supporter spilling over into the graffiti of protest versus the state, against the establishment, of anti-Welsh officialdom.

To add to the confusion, as we drove out of the car park, someone threw a handful of gravel at the car as we drove down Mold Road, back home to Prestatyn. A group of young men who threw the stones, and had presumably daubed the cock and balls, ran after the car, that thankfully had the horsepower to get us out of there, Starsky and

Hutch style. It was an interesting experience.

Nurse Kearns reads this and smiles. "That's a real detailed recall" she says, making a note of this. "This is real progress. Had did you feel the next morning. Can you remember?"

I sink back into the past and think hard.

"I felt sad, I always felt sad when we lost, like a weird sinking feeling in my tummy."

The memory hovers for the moment. I'm in a different space and time. I can recall minor details. The duvet cover on my bed is covered in the Wrexham Badge and colours. Posters on a wall of players, Dixie McNeil, Steve Fox, a team photo, trophies proudly displayed.

She appears really pleased with me. This makes me feel good. I have another memory I mention. I don't wait for her to answer. I told her about Chelsea away.

It was the early 1980s. It was my first away game. Stamford Bridge London. League Division 2. Before the Premier League. This was the second tier of English football. My dad took me. We met my uncle, a police constable in the Metropolitan Police.

We stood in a section for families, a terrace with barriers you could lean against. To my right were the Wrexham fans, penned in like sheep, huge fences at the front of the terrace to keep them in. To my left, a section of Chelsea fans, their tops off, skin covered in tattoos with National Front and symbols of swastikas and bulldogs and the union jack.

The atmosphere was hostile. I was terrified. I'd never experienced such a display of hatred between humans. It felt like a battle in a war. The game was an irrelevance. It was difficult to enjoy. We drew 2-2. I remember Joey Jones giving a salute of a fist in the air to the Wrexham supporters at the end of the game.

Dr Paskin makes a note of this. She smiles. It's time for some sleep, she says. The rest will fuel the recovery. I close my eyes. Behind my eyelids is an overflowing bowl of images, memories, fantasies, dreams, things that have never happened, things that might have happened.

My mind is racing. I'm handed my medication. I swallow this and feel my heart rate slowing, I feel a wave of calmness, tranquility, a feeling that everything might just be getting better. I fall into a deep and heavy dreamless sleep.

Day 4, 2030

The morning is bright and cold, the sky low and grey, a faint sun, with an apocalyptic quality to it. A shimmer of starlings on a telephone line settles for a while before dispersing into the clear colourless sky. There's something incredibly soothing about the murmuration of starlings. I could watch them for hours; drifting, dancing, resting, exploding as a collective.

For what feels like a few moments, I watch the space outside the window for a minute, waiting for something to fill the space, the time. Nothing however comes, just the distant rattle of a train, morning traffic, lines of taillights, the endless drone, taking the dead-eyed commuters to their awful pods to waste away another day in their bland existence, chasing the dollar, climbing the ladder, following the dream, another day in their personal paradise, what they may, later in life accept as a living hell.

The nurse from the night before comes in, checks out the machines, makes some notes, brings in a tray and parks it on a bedside cabinet. She's different today. No makeup. No Mars Bar eyebrows, normal lashes, no lips of a trout. She doesn't smile. Makes no eye contact. She looks pretty and I just wish she could understand that she doesn't need that shit and that image of what beauty is, from whoever it is, making the rules, making her think like that is how she needs to be.

I try and imagine a life for her away from here but all I can produce is an empty apartment with a bed and a TV and a fridge and a small hob for cooking. I see everyone beyond a life I imagine and wonder if this is a consequence of head trauma or is it something everyone considers. She leaves the room heavy footed. Dr Paskin replaces her, looking vibrant and charismatic and her life is I imagine, rich with love, objects, warmth, and empathy.

Did you sleep well she might ask? She would smile as she speaks. Lifelines creasing around eyes and cheeks. She would place a hand on my shoulder. She will make sense of all this. My beautiful saviour. The physio will be with you after your breakfast, she would say. I might nod. I might do nothing. Sometimes doing nothing is vastly underrated.

Today has the quality of how I imagine it is aboard a submarine. A nothingness in the substance of the air, a heavy thud in the gaps between things, objects, people. I'm about to be unveiled, to come out of the void, to rise out of the inky abyss.

Dr Paskin hugged me warmly and I detected a smudge of tear in her eyes, but she hides it with a heavy blink, and I retain the hug for longer than I believe she intended. There's a legacy of some perfume she might have worn last night at a social event with a boyfriend at a fancy restaurant. I prefer not to dwell on this, instead wondering about the future, knowing Dr Paskin most probably won't be part of that.

I recall I hate goodbyes, maybe everyone does. But for me it's deep. I feel a surge of nausea swilling in my gut at the thought of change, saying farewell, the end of something rather than the start of something potentially much better than it is, this, what I have, a room, a space, sparse memories.

Not remembering much before this, just fractures of feelings and slithers of memories is both horrendous, absurd, and yet, strangely cathartic. There's an element of a clean slate, factory settings. I can be whatever I want to be. There's part of this where I don't want to learn about my former pre-coma life. There's another where I want to know everything.

I met today's trainer, Mike Muldoon. He used to be a footballer. He has the walk, the confident stride of an athlete. He told me about a fitness plan. We do some gentle warmups to assess my fitness. A five-minute run, a row, some stretches, a couple of burpees. He says we'll start properly tomorrow.

After my shower and a contemplated, aborted attempt at masturbation, (one negative of memory loss being a redundant wank-bank), the footage they put on the Big TV is of a toddler and a baby. There's a woman, broadly familiar, and then me, wearing swimming trunks, looking a bit chubbier than I am now and yeah, I get it, having a coma to get in shape is extreme but I'd look better in those trunks in that scene now that's for sure. This must be me. I'm a father? A husband?

Dr Paskin leaves the room. I pick up a spoon and play about with the bowl of porridge one of the caterers has brought for me, submerging blueberries beneath the sticky surface. I trickle some honey from one of those cartons you get on an airplane meal, peeling it open with an awkwardness, disproportionate to the size of this condiment, as a child kicks you over and over in the back of your seat. And you want to kick the crap out of the little shit.

Dr Paskin returns and pours water into a cup and hands me my meds, two tone tablets in red and orange. Pretty little things. Like Tic-Tacs. Here, drink this, she would say. I oblige and then accept an offer of a coffee, black and without sugar. I drink it whilst it's at its hottest, letting the sour coffee scold my tongue - that feeling of extreme hot or cold, where extremes meet, almost impossible to distinguish.

The mug has an image of a superhero in a red suit with the strapline beneath it saying: 'Love is a beautiful thing. When you find it, the whole world tastes like Daffodil Daydream.'

On the Big TV, an advertisement for a vacuum cleaner, an improbably beautiful homemaker sitting at a breakfast bar chatting to other beautiful homemakers, the vacuum cleaner whirring around the room picking up dust and general household debris. There's no one pushing it, no wires, cables and then a feature for a robot on the outside of the window, cleaning it. No platforms, no equipment, no humans; the world of cleaning has moved on.

The homemakers look otherworldly and I'm not sure if they are human or holographic images, or some form of advanced animated state. They're strangely asexual, perfect, and ugly, alien-like. They are a combination of men, women and the in-between.

Dr Paskin asks if I would meet Dr Salathiel. He's already in the room so it's not really a choice she's giving me. He's standing there in his white coat. He doesn't look like a doctor. He doesn't sound like a doctor. It's because he looks like a fucking schoolkid with his bum fluff, his floppy hair, and thick nerdy glasses. He looks like he should be an extra in a Harry Potter movie.

I might ask him if he knows what he's doing and does his parents know he's out here on his own as he runs a hand through his quiff and then the wispy hair growing in clasps from pale cheeks. He half smiles and writes something into an iPad and exits the room saying something towards a colleague in the entrance to the room.

I focus on the sky colour through the one window in my room, a shallow grey texture to it, with a hint of pink and pale yellow over the low hills that spread beyond the row of unremarkable buildings. Oozes of smoke rise from chimneys on an industrial estate, a shift in the tone of the afternoon, as cars drift across the motorway in the half distance heading out of town, to other places, elsewhere.

In the office block opposite, the outline of a silhouette of a man, his face lit up by the glow of a computer screen. A human-sized body shape stands and hovers behind this person, pointing something towards the screen, a pen, its nib alternating between columns of endless data that appear on the screen. The man withdraws the pen, shakes his head, before disappearing inevitably, middle manager like, into another pod.

There's a cactus in this office scene, some photos in awful novelty frames of children on a pier, post-it notes dotted around his oblong existence covered with infinite minutiae: a feeling of endless, hellish futility seeping through the air conditioning that keeps him and his colleagues from internally combusting and realising, if they thought about it, that this is no way to live.

I remember something about work, the early mornings, the routine, the commute, late trains, traffic jams, gridlock, life sapping inch-creep lines of traffic, road rage, selfish fuckers blocking yellow boxes. Extreme, unfathomable rage. The slacks and shirts, people in shit suits and even shitter ties. A feeling of utter futility. A life wasted.

Dr Paskin, sensing my melancholy and despair about the possible tedium of a former life, directs the Big TV to 'Play.'

2022

The Queen is dead. The republicans celebrate. The monarchists, how they mourn. The BBC shows no other news, just interviews will people queuing to see the dead Queen on an endless loop. There's other stuff going on naturally, as other stuff doesn't just miraculously stop when a monarch dies.

A war in Ukraine, an energy crisis, a new prime minister, and chancellor policy making by tossing a coin. It's sad, of course, everyone will concede, but a 96-year-old passing away isn't wildly unpredictable and the coverage feels more totalitarian regime than constitutional monarchy.

There a flurry of undercurrent gathering for Independence in Wales and Scotland and the new monarch King Charles appears to have missed the mood by renewing the Prince of Wales position, traditionally seen as a symbol of English oppression, bestowing the title upon his son, who claims a tepid bond from living and having a couple of pints on Anglesey when he lived there for a couple of years.

Football matches are scrapped whilst cricket and rugby, traditionally the sport of the elite, carry on unaffected. There's an unease building not helped by Liz Truss, the new prime minister announcing a series of financial measures that serve to stoke the flames of discontent amongst the working classes with tax cuts for the highest earners and the scrapping of caps on bonuses. The socio-political landscape is a volatile tinderbox, waiting to ignite.

Wrexham F.C. lost 5-4 to Grimsby Town F.C. in a thrilling Play Off Semi Final.

The new documentary series on Disney +, 'Welcome to Wrexham' is well received with a growing interest in the fifth-tier non-league club across the world.

Day 5, 2030

The man who gives me my meds this morning has googly eyes, a dog like quality about him. I asked him a question about COVID-19 and whether he was around for the pandemic. He doesn't answer and I don't push it, instead mentioning the sunrise this morning; colours I'd never seen before is how I put it.

I've noticed that COVID-19 is something which you don't talk about. It appears to have left an indelible stain on the fabric of the people I am interacting with here. There's a lowering of the gaze, a brief collision of eye contact, room exits. Nobody wants to discuss the pandemic. 2020 really does appear to have been a shit-show.

I gulp down the tablets, four or five of them, helping them down with a tumbler of water that the man must have handed me. His jaw clicks as he watches me, that makes me feel slightly nauseous.

I can remember my appearance from when I last looked in a mirror, took a selfie. I imagine I've aged more than a decade. They'll be a greyness beyond my eyes, a dull tone to my skin that isn't quite a colour anymore.

All this that happened whilst I slept, dead, dreamless: fed by tubes, machines, and computers that were increasingly doing the things we humans would tend to do before, more than ten years ago. A lifetime, a generation, half a generation - a decade of restoration, to fix, to patch up the decay that had gone before.

People inevitably passed whilst I slept. Films have been made, books written, former presidents assassinated, marriages broken, new lives born. Waking from a coma gives you some fresh perspective, that's for sure. You'd have to be some psycho not to have been changed by the experience.

In my Dream Session, I tell Dr Paskin I was on an island alone and desperately lonely and that my only company was a coconut that I would carry around with me. She notes this down and asks me if there was anything else, is there anyone else you specifically remember, that may have featured in your dreams.

I think hard and gulp on some Lucozade and tell her, there was one about me playing football, making my debut for Wales and I was in the changing room with Gareth Bale and others and then I'm singing the anthem and then I'm scoring a last gasp winner to qualify for the World Cup.

She asks me how that made me feel and I say truly joyous and euphoric and it's just a shame to wake up and realise it hadn't happened and it will never happen and it's probably a bit like dreaming someone who died is alive or of a lover who dumped you and you are together again only briefly in that dream like state. I recall I wrote a book when I was a kid about me playing for Wales and Wrexham. It's all I wanted to do.

It's a desolate feeling for sure I say. Like life is elsewhere. As if I'm the only person in the universe. A dream unfulfilled can be one of the worst feelings in the world.

She says we should leave it there and I think about telling her about the recurring dream of the hammerhead shark people and the living head of Donald Trump in a jar in my cellar, that Brett Ormerod miss in the play-off final against Newport, but I decide against it. She closes her iPad and in a calm and compelling voice, is telling me to watch the Big TV.

111

I look across the room, take in the scene, my surroundings, the equipment, the austere landscape, the white blank canvas of sky perfectly framed, the sheer blankness of everything. I am, I suppose, trying to keep my vision clear of the vulgar screen of the Big TV that fills the entirety of the wall. Is this what you all watch your shit on nowadays?

I have a memory blast of televisions from my past, a deep comical box in the corner of a room, larger than an armchair, moving on to something a bit slimmer on a metal futuristic stand, then something on moveable bracket in the corner of a kitchen, then something thinner, hung on a wall; now this, a bank of screens, built into a wall. The evolution of our viewing pleasure is like a Darwinian diagram, I picture in my head.

I can avoid it no longer and I adjust my posture ready to view the stuff they want me to see. The well-worn instruction to buzz when you recognise anything, she reminds me. Yeah, you mentioned it I say, blankly, without expression. I watch the Big TV.

There's some more pandemic stuff, lots of footage of people walking along in facemasks, chaotic hospital scenes, Boris Johnson press conferences, flanked by medical experts looking stressed and deadly seriously as they work through absurdly basic looking graphs and slides.

I'm buzzing at a fair few of these scenes; memories pricked at, snatches of time together - millions and billions of shards of moments, milliseconds, images, components, sentences, dialogues, all coming together, bulldozed around as a giant kaleidoscope you might have had as a child. I just don't know, right here, right now, if they'll ever be laid out in a sequence that is cohesive, that makes sense, like a vast domino trail to be exploded in a Guinness world record attempt.

There's some football footage, a game of rugby, a golfer teeing off on an immaculate course. Endless ribbons of sports results, newscasters, robotic looking with plump lips and heavy eyebrows like chocolate bars, a graphic of an architect's drawing for a futuristic football stadium, part of which is vaguely familiar.

She directs the Big TV to blink off and tells me it's gym time which is something of a relief. The physio, Gary Shinton, gave me a fitness test, a sprint on an incredibly futuristic treadmill. It's of course futuristic to a man who's been lying in a bed for nearly ten years. It's probably the staple for 2030.

You don't notice incremental change. It just happens, evolves, day by day. The ageing process, weight gain, technology. But for me, I'd perhaps notice these shifts: the creases around my eyes, the grey around my temples, my stubble, the gym equipment, the coffee machines, the vacuum cleaners, everything controlled by voice recognition.

The physio leans over, and the incline shifts one percent every minute and I'm within five minutes, properly fucked, wiped out, jelly fish legs, a feeling of nausea leaking in my throat. In my defence, I've been laid out on my arse for ten years so to get to five minutes isn't bad. But I'm sweating like a pig in a blanket and the plastic cup of water that Carlos hands me is delicious.

I recall the ten thousand step mantra pre-coma, but it was nothing more than a marketing slogan with Fitbit, a step measuring device. Things have moved on a little. Steps are monitored centrally and life insurance, tax allowances, holiday entitlements, benefits, are all intrinsically linked to the number of steps recorded on a device implanted into a chip in your arm.

By all accounts after the pandemic, it became clear that obesity was a huge burden on the health system that was, to an extent, to the government, a controllable. With a suitable incentive, some people could be encouraged to be more active and lose weight, was the view politicians took from their trusted Oxbridge advisors.

Through my window, a light from the office opposite blinks on. The computer screen throws a triangular glow that outlines the back of a man's head. He's navigating his desktop. His right arm bends and twists. His jawbone drops and rises. He stands. I want him so much to turn. I need for some reason to see his face. I need to know if he matches my expectations. I need some certainty.

The screen falls dark. The room slips into a shade of dark pavement grey. Outlines of other objects slightly darker than the airspace that is left. Office furniture. Unremarkable desks. Minimal equipment. Everything seems in this future that has been dumped upon me, to be lesser than it was before. The world is becoming less cluttered, more streamlined.

Still surveying this view, remnants of a light from an adjoining corridor disappear and everything slips into darkness. I turn away from the window and try to sleep but Dr Paskin says we need to see what happened in 2023 and 2024. She directs the Big TV to 'Play.'

2023

Wrexham F.C. finally achieved, fifteen years to the day they fell out of the league pyramid, promotion back to the football league after an emotional 3-1 victory at home to Boreham Wood. Manager Phil Parkinson remarked: "I'm incredibly proud to be the manager that has taken this wonderful club back to where it belongs. We are going to achieve some fantastic things if we stick together and do things the right way."

A week later, for the last game of the season, Torquay is painted red and white and Philadelphia green as the fans celebrate something they perhaps had secretly feared would never ever happen in their lifetime, or indeed, in any lifetime, followed on the Tuesday evening by an incredible spectacle, an open top bus parade with thousands lining the streets of Wrexham.

Amidst the celebratory scenes, it's difficult to imagine the club had once almost died and only the fierce loyalty of the supporters and its town had saved it from the clutches of hideous businessmen; vile asset strippers who didn't care about heritage, about something intrinsically linked to the community it's part of.

There's a lot that is wrong about football, but this is a story about good defeating evil, that greed and power do not always succeed. The media rightly see this as a good news story. The coverage is intense, across the world, Wrexham is becoming a global brand. The reports of a fairy tale, the stardust of Hollywood, a script you just couldn't write, flash across news screens across the world.

Owners Rob and Ryan are heralded as the savours of the club. Rightly, it is pointed out that those involved with the Supporters Trust - the previous custodians of the club, it should never be forgotten - had managed to stabilise the finances and provide and create a culture of a community feel to the club again.

They provided a platform for there to be a club that was interesting and viable enough to be approached for a takeover. This should never be forgotten and those involved should also always be proud of the role they played. The celebrations in the city and the region go on for weeks. Nobody can wait for the new season to start.

Wrexham band Declan Swans are number one in the charts with a new song, It's Always Sunny in Wrexham which has become a terrace anthem. The band also support Kings of Leon in a sold-out concert at the Racecourse Ground.

2024

Joe Wicks stands for election at a hastily arranged by-election after the sudden death of Tory MP XXXXXX XXXXXXX (name retracted for legal reasons) and wins by a landslide.

The likeable Essex Fitness Guru declaring, "I'm going to make Britain fitter, not fatter" puts forward a new white paper for a tax system partially based on the number of steps a person expends and the calories a person consumes. Support for the proposal gathers pace as the electorate appreciates the pressures COVID-19 put on the NHS.

Wrexham F.C. start the season with five straight wins. New striker, Dewi Davies from Llanfaethlu, Anglesey, makes his debut after coming through the youth ranks after being spotted doing keep-me-ups on Borthwen Beach. He quickly reaches double figures and is widely heralded as the new 'Ian Rush.' On hearing the comparison, Rushie, the legendary former Wales, and Liverpool striker says:

"Well, he's an exciting prospect I'd say. And it's great that he's not from a foreign country, unless you class Anglesey as foreign, that is."

F.C. Romans of Chester City (2024) are born: the phoenix club who rose from the ruins of the failed phoenix club that had previously risen, ultimately unsuccessfully from the original, Chester F.C. who to be fair had been in existence for some years and who had produced legends such as Ian Rush and Stuart Rimmer and Paul Rutherford.

The creation of this new club is announced in a glittering press conference, the new owner announced from a video link from Hollywood, Hugh Jackman, dressed as his character, Wolverine. The arch-rival of Ryan Reynolds' Deadpool, it appears that the reason for the take-over, was the fierce rivalry between near neighbours Chester and Wrexham, two clubs only 13 miles apart, the border between England and Wales running between the clubs, adding some spice to the local rivalry. Mr. Jackman declares:

"I'm going to smash you Deadpool. And we're going to smash you Wrexham."

Fights break out in Chester city centre that night between rival supporters of Wrexham and Chester, many dressed as Marvel superhero characters. Police make several arrests, including three Deadpool's, a Hulk, a Wolverine and a confused Zippy from Rainbow who mistakenly thought he was attending a Children's Retro TV Show Convention.

A Wrexham F.C. statement reads: Whilst we regret the social disturbance in Blacon last night, we confirm the violence was perpetrated by our English neighbours and our supporters were acting in self-defence. We only wish we could do battle again on the football pitch, but we can't envisage this happening anytime soon.

#yourejustasmalltowninwales
#shitgroundnofans
#whatsitliketoseeacrowd

Deadpool 3 comes out to rave reviews. A new character, Wreck-EM, joins the main protagonists' group of do-gooders: half dragon, half man, he breathes fire, speaks with a North-Walian accent, and generally loves engaging anyone about football and the rule relating to offside, a concept that, like so many things, many North Americans unfathomably struggle to understand.

Paul Mullin, Wrexham's star striker, makes a cameo role, scoring an overhead kick in a five a side game between several super-heroes, in the film's closing scene.

It's Always Sunny in Philadelphia launches series 20, or whatever series it is up to nowadays. Rob McElhenney and the bar staff in Paddy's Bar adopt a new uniform, Wrexham F.C.'s new, replica kit sponsored by Joe Wicks.

After a brief relationship, Madonna dumps Donald Trump who immediately sues her for breaching his copyright in her new single: Like a Virgin (Version 2024) in which an image of Donald Trump in a wedding dress on a gondola in Venice as a parody of the original 1983 single becomes an internet sensation.

Bear Grylls announces he'll be running for MP for Gwynedd in next year's election. Rumours that local councillors were promised a part in his new documentary series in return for his new man-made island off the coast of Abersoch, receiving unopposed planning permission, are strenuously denied.

Bear, hanging from a cliff face on a previously unclimbed summit in Antarctica, declines to comment, instead tweeting the words 'island life' with a picture of Bear holding onto the dorsal fins of two bottle nosed dolphins as they carry him through the Irish Sea, his new island in the background beneath a low blue sky.

Donald Trump survives another assassination attempt whilst visiting F.C. East Fife in Scotland, when during their 5-4 victory over Forfar Athletic (think about it), a local landowner attempts to shoot him with a crossbow. Narrowly missing his vital organs, the former President, lost his left arm during the attack. Local surgeon, Mackintosh Macdonald says the decision to amputate was 'touch and go' but after tossing a coin, and then a game of Rock, Paper, Scissors, it was unanimously decided that out with the surgical saw was the way to go.

Gareth Bale comes out of retirement and signs for Wrexham F.C. Even by the standards of the audacious League 2 club, this is a major coup, and only serves to further propel the club into the international spotlight. Turning up for the announcement and subsequent press conference, he's spotted carrying his coveted golf bag, and once the formalities are sorted, he's rumoured to be playing 18 holes with Rob and Ryan.

The top-knotted Welsh legend says he's looking forward to playing his part in taking Wrexham up the leagues, as well as discovering the wonderful golf courses north Wales has to offer.

Elon Musk announces a Spaceflight into outer space. It is rumoured that his co astronaut will be Donald Trump.

Joe Wicks, launches a new brand of athletic wear called 'Joe Wicks Athletic Wear.'

Greta Thunberg is photographed eating a Big Mac in Stockholm. Resisting an injunction that Greta's team attempt to obtain to block the story, Rupert Murdoch employs a team of private detectives who obtain DNA from a bin outside the fast-food outlet and provide documentary evidence that it was in fact a Big Mac, with cheese. The headlines are brutal.

Greenpeace and V, a new fast food Vegan franchise that she had become the face of, immediately withdraw from their contractual arrangement with her, citing 'brand and cultural inconsistencies.'

It is also reported (unsubstantiated) that the Environmental Teen-Warrior was also spotted buying a pack of streaky (smoked) bacon from a Lidl outside the Danish town of Lyngby.
Prince Andrew faces legal action that could lead him being extradited to New York to face trial for sex offences linked to sex offender Jeffrey

Epstein. Ex-girlfriend, former professional badminton player, Jemimah Shuttle-Cocker said, 'he always had an eye for a young girl, the sweaty bastard.'

Ex wife Sarah Ferguson says: "He wasn't known as Randy-Andy for nothing."

Danny DeVito, is spotted at a press conference for the new series of It's Always Sunny in Philadelphia, wearing a T-shirt with Joe Wicks rising from a burpee saying: "I'm going to make you fitter, not fatter."

North Korean Supreme Leader, Kim Jong-Un is assassinated whilst out drinking with Donald Trump and Madonna. It's unclear, according to news agency Reuter's, whether he was the intended target of the incendiary device, planted under a disabled toilet at Richard Branson's retreat where the group were holidaying.

His Majesty's hairpiece was found on the ceiling of the exclusive Wash Closet and stories of the ink black wig, made from the fur of a black panther, being sold on the black market for millions of dollars have not been substantiated.

Rumours also abound that the intended target was in fact, Donald Trump, who did lose an arm in the explosion. Madonna emerges unscathed but for a pair of laddered tights.

North Korea moves quickly to bring in Wham Bam Bum as the new Supreme Leader, nephew of Kim Jong-Un, and a recent graduate of Eton and Oxford University where he studied Philosophy, Politics and Economics, and mixed socially, it is rumoured, with Boris Johnson and most of the rest of the Tory Party.

University President, Rupert Bartholomew Reese Mog Wank-Stain, tweets:

"Good luck to Wham Bam Bum in his new role. He will be missed by our rugby team: he was a quite splendid right-winger."

Wham Bam Bum is pictured in a propaganda video, driving a military vehicle in a vast military parade, carrying a nuclear warhead whilst wearing the new all black third kit of Wrexham F.C., sponsored by vegan coffee shop chain, The Jaunty Goat.

There's a feeling that the new regime might display a more liberal approach, moving forwards.

Dr Paskin directs the Big TV to switch off. We play Connect 4 and after beating her 10-0, we call it a night.

Day 6, 2030

In the night, a storm booms above the town, echoing through distant hills and valleys. Lightning cracks open the sky, illuminating buildings and streets and fields. There's a tension in the air that comes with a storm, a pent-up energy, a feeling of energy and release.

During breakfast I have a memory blast of a football match I might have, pre-coma, attended. Dr Paskin makes a note of this in her iPad, whilst sipping on a coffee. In my memory, there's a low building with feeble floodlights at either corner, a breeze block construction, mightily unimpressive.

If you were an alien visiting your first human football match, you would be feeling distinctly underwhelmed. Approaching the 'stadium' there's a heaviness to the air, a stench of tension and compressed energy, a powder keg of a segment of society looking for a release, an escape from the mundanity of their everyday existence, an opportunity to be someone in this gang of like-minded thuggery.

As I take a bite from a cantaloupe melon, dip a raspberry into a fine white yogurt that has the appearance of a silky lake, I recall in this memory blast, the eruption of a mass brawl on a street, tens of youths wearing the go-to make of the day, Stone Island jackets, Adidas trainers, jeans by Giorgio

Armani.

They're all similar, clones of each other, dressed the same, saying the same stuff, gesturing the same, all shouting songs to each other, frantically looking like they want to get to the opponent whilst being held apart by a line of policeman dressed heavily in riot gear.

There's the sounds of dogs, chanting, the smell of onion and grease, beer glasses shattering on the concrete floor. There's a suspicion as to whether they would do anything if the police weren't there. It's a game between Chester and Wrexham. I remember this.

I finished my breakfast. I go to the gymnasium. It's a new trainer today, Steve Massey-Ferguson. He's heavily built, like a shit house from brick. He's a bit of a twat. You can tell that from his demeanour, his tone, his language. Maybe he's trying to play the old school colonel routine; this doesn't work for me. People management is all about deducing what your audience needs to tick, to get the best out of people.

The session is intense. Mountain climbers, burpees, squat holds, burpee squats, goblet squat holds, a one-legged burpee, sit ups, shoulder tap planks, and then a tedious 60-minute row. The secret is to keep your back straight, done a certain way, you can still gather steps, is the biggest tip of the day. I drink water. I do more lunges and burpees and then hill sprints again. These exercises might be familiar for you but for me, they're completely new.

My fitness will recover quicker than I think he says. You must be patient, he says. Ah fuck you I mutter with your ripped arms and your washboard stomach. Lying in a coma for a decade hasn't done wonders for my six-pack. He says he'll see me next week and I go off for my shower, writing in the condensation. I sing something. Karma Chameleon by Culture Club – the first single I ever bought perhaps?

Your brain will recover memories, at random. Our job is to piece them all together, says Dr Paskin. You just need to keep it slow, don't push it too much, it'll all come with time.

We do a crossword together. I finished it in under half an hour. My knowledge is staggering. Nine down, conker loving board game obsessive: chess-nut. Medieval comedian - rhymes with non-league football team: Jester.

Dr Paskin tells me I need to watch the Big TV. Press this buzzer every time a memory is triggered, she reminds me:

Footage on the screen of a football match. There's a team in yellow, the other in red, the officials in black. The floodlights throw out a light that seems to hang heavy in the cold night as a patch of mist might do above a lake or a low tide.

Around the pitch, advertising boards with Minera Roof Trusses, Gola, Abbey National. Stewards in yellow jackets sit on absurd plastic chairs. Cigarette smoke rises above the crowd, rammed into the stands and steep, overflowing terraces.

There's a feeling that this scene playing out, beneath planets, satellites, comets, parallel universes mirroring this, is the centre of the universe for everyone here to witness this.

There's a real sense of euphoria when a man with a mullet that might be more at home in a bar in North Dakota, scores from a free kick, the ball sailing in the top corner of the net. If an alien were watching this, they'd be perplexed by the scene unfolding; large groups of humans jumping on each other, gripping faces, smacking backs. Some are sat on a grey concrete floor, heads in hands, tears coming out of bloodshot, disbelieving eyes.

Behind the goal, where the ball has settled, the crowd in the main don't respond, apart from a few people in yellow coats spread about the aisles. The camera that is depicting this scene pans around the other sides of the crowd where the audience is a throng of celebration.

I press my buzzer. I remember this.

Then, a man with short blond hair scuppers the ball past the man in green who tries to reach it with an outstretched hand.

I press my buzzer. I remember this, I shout.

Dr Paskin gestures to the buzzer. You need to concentrate, she says.

Still watching the Big TV, the referee blows into a whistle and a shrill tone bringing the participants on this oblong of grass to a halt. They exchange hands, some hug, others collapse to the ground, gripping cold frosting turf in their hands.

I press my buzzer.

If you were an alien being exposed to this activity for the first time, you might have it described to you as follows: This by all accounts is sport. A sub section of this is football where twenty-two people aim to kick a ball into a net. Sports interest humans.

People who can play elite sport get paid more money than anyone, even surgeons who work to save human life. It's an odd paradox that being able to do something so abstract is so celebrated throughout society. These acts, the sport, the images that have played out, scratch at a memory, a faint trickle of something, a euphoria that feels at this moment, highly irrational and irrelevant.

I am now, the metaphoric alien, seeing the world through the lens of an outsider, unfamiliar with the everyday, that I used to exist within, oblivious to, just drifting through.

Dr Paskin smiles faintly. There's the stench of some root vegetable boiled in an industrial kitchen. On the Big TV, an image of the man with the mullet, freeze-framed, his face immortalised in this glorious moment, in human history. Oh, to be so revered, to be so relevant to so many, for so long, maybe forever.

I keep pressing my buzzer, over and over.

I fucking remember this I say. I fucking remember the man who scored the winner, Stevie fucking Watkin - never gets the credit that lad deserves what with the Mickey T free-kick. The words hurtle from my mouth. I have no idea how, but I remember this.

I recall playing Culture Club, putting a poster of them on my bedroom wall next to a flag with the Wrexham crest on it, a team photo from Shoot magazine, a poster of Joey Jones clenching his fist to an overspilling Kop. Ollie Kearns, John Paskin, Phil Hardy, Gary Bennett, Neil Ashton, these random names keep spilling from my gaping hole of a mouth. More come dripping out, Ben Tozer, Jon Bowden, Steve Massey, Paul Mullin.

Dr Paskin sprints from the room. There's not enough time for anything to happen by the time she's back, an army of her medical colleagues hampering my air space, pulling down my eyes, hooking me up to a machine that links to a screen where images of a brain are looked at by two men who muffle an exchange of conversation, nodding, half nodding, generally being all secretive and scientific, overspilling with menace and fuckery.

All I can do is picture this scene of this football match, a feeling of elation, smells of fatty hot dogs and onions, steam coming out of vents of the hut where men pissed, some in sinks, some over the legs of others, but nobody cared. In a landscape where Bovril-breathed men hugged and kept saying we beat the fucking Arsenal; we only went and beat the fucking Arsenal - no one minded the piss of another running down his leg.

An alien indeed would, regardless of their status of perhaps being light years more developed than us, be perplexed by these absurd activities and might be compelled to return from where they have come, to report back to their superiors of this brutal, backward orb, where the natives are just too strange to even begin to conquer and colonise.

Dr Paskin turns off the Big TV with a verbal command. She tells me I've done well. It's been a big day, she says. I say something back to her in Icelandic that means, I appreciate all your help and compassion. It's useful being multi-lingual.

I fell into a deep sleep. Outside, it rains. Lorries drive along roads carrying goods to depots, delivery men taking stuff to shops. Society keeps functioning whilst I lie in my bed, my brain recovering, my dreams playing out like a crazy projector in an absurd cinema where the only audience is me.

Day 7, 2030

This is what I wrote in my Dream Book. It's the first thing I do after taking a sip of water from a tumbler placed on the side table by my bed:

'A man running down the aisles of a supermarket, an Aldi, I think it is, wearing an octopus on his head, as if it's an absurd hair piece. He's going down the frozen food aisle and he's shouting 'where are the garden peas' over and over and a shop worker, a shelf stacker, I suppose you would call them, is trying to rugby tackle the man but keeps missing and falling on the floor as the man keeps charging up the aisle towards the Asian foods section where he smashes open a bottle of oyster sauce that spills all over the floor. An Astronaut comes from behind a stack of Golden Graham's and starts shooting laser beams at the man and he hits a woman behind the cheese counter as she cuts up a circle of Gouda and falls to the ground like an extra in Platoon or a diving Harry Kane or Raheem Sterling and shouts, 'Brie, I love you, Brie.' I also mention Brett Ormerod missing a chance against Newport County at Wembley in a play-off final which seems to be a recurring nightmare.

"That's it", I say to Dr Paskin. "That's my dream".

She asks if that really was my dream, and I say, do you really think I'd go to the effort of making all that up, and she stares at me saying nothing which I take as her thinking I did make it up and she's right, I did (apart from the Brett Ormerod part which did really happen). I rather dreamt of me and Dr Paskin having sex on the side of a volcano as molten magma shot all over the sky and fork lightning lit up the horizon.

I decided not to disclose this. I'm still my own fucking man, despite this circus I live in, I want you to know that. She asks if there's anything more. I say I had the recurring hammerhead shark bullshit, where my whole town turns into hammerhead sharks, but wear human clothes and take on the features of people I know; people I walk past, work with, see down the pub.

Some wear hats, some three-piece suits, there's even a vicar with a white collar and a policeman wearing a police hat over his vast hammerhead. She nods and I say, yes, I keep having the hammerhead shark dream. And then there's Margaret Thatcher and the living head of Donald Trump in a jar in my cellar. Blah, blah, Blah.

She seems keen to move on and directs the Big TV to 'Play.'

2025

Ukraine's President is Guest of Honour at Wrexham's opening game of the season and officially cuts the red and white ribbon signifying the opening of the New Kop Stand, replacing the terracing that had lay derelict for decades.

A capacity crowd of 17,500 witness a 7-0 victory over Salford United, a team bank-rolled for years by a Singaporean businessman and some former Manchester United players.

When Wrexham were struggling, Salford would be able to entice players who Wrexham were trying to sign, paying inflated wages. Commentators argue that these are the types of teams, those without a history or a fan base are the true 'tinpot' clubs who aren't good for the game. Salford fans ironically sing to their Wrexham counterparts, 'where were you when you were shit.'

Deadpool 4 has been released. Paul Mullen plays a new superhero, The Red Dragon, who can breathe fire and helps the oppressed and terrorises the privileged elite. Goalkeeper Ben Foster, who has signed a new three-year contract, is rumoured to be in rehearsals for Deadpool 5.

Vladimir Putin is assassinated whilst doing a stadium tour in Siberia. New President Nicholas Gorbachev, grandson of the 1980s reformist Mikael, is appointed as his immediate successor and like his grandfather, he has a zeal for reform, immediately announcing there will be a new dawn in Russia, with his first act being an immediate withdrawal and apology to the people of Ukraine.

In other news, the Republican movement in the UK is given a boost with the death of King Charles. The cause of death is unclear, with rumours being he died of food poisoning. One of the royal chefs, Hamish Sturgeon, is taken in for questioning but is later released without charge. A post-mortem is inconclusive.

President Gorbachev attends the last game of Wrexham's season with President Zelensky, the two of them paraded on the pitch before the title decider against Tranmere Rovers.

Ben Foster, at 44 years old, saves a last-minute penalty, with Paul Mullin, now himself approaching veteran status, scoring in injury time, the winner, his 250th goal for Wrexham, after a wonderful dribble from his own area by Welsh legend and golfer, Gareth Bale.

Following the death of King Charles, Mark Drakeford, keen to fight off the people's candidate, enigmatic actor Michael Sheen, who has announced he wants to stand for Mr. Drakeford's position, is somewhere in the hospitality section eating prawn wontons wearing a 'king is dead' t shirt. He turns his back on the minutes silence, which is largely ignored, with much of the crowd, staying outside the ground, demonstrating via a 'silent protest.'

It's three years since the death of his mother Queen Elizabeth, when the country went into a North Korean-esq shutdown. People were told not to watch football. People were instead told to mourn, as an endless stream of expensively tedious ceremonies took place.

On social media, there's all sorts of arguments and counter arguments about the monarchy and socialism and the tourism argument that seems to be used by many as a reason for its continuance. Someone mentions that France earns more from people visiting its royal palaces without the expense of having a royal family.

Donald Trump survives another assassination attempt whilst visiting Scotland but suffers further life-changing injuries, after a man runs amok on his tractor, on the outskirts of Dumbarton, colliding into Trump and his entourage who were playing golf on a nearby course recently developed by the former president.

Archie McSporran, local dairy farmer, and lifelong Dumbarton F.C. season ticket holder was said to be incensed by the plans submitted to the local planning authority to demolish Dumbarton F.C. as well as two thirds of his farm, to develop the new Trump Golf and Conference Centre.

When interviewed by the local constabulary, the local farmer was reported as saying:

"Yes, when I heard the news (of the planning application), I went out, milked the herd, had some breakfast, told the wife I had some business in town, got in my Massey Ferguson (tractor), drove over to the local golf course that Trump has also acquired, cut through the path the greenkeeper Angus McPherson-McFlurrie uses to get to the large series of bunkers between the 9th and 10th holes (Angus is a good friend and fellow opponent of the proposed Trump Development) and set about mowing Trump down."

He went on: "I went for the balls, if I'm honest" he said to reporters from the Dumbarton Weekly. "I put on the blades of my combine harvester and went straight for the bollocks. His bodyguard took the brunt of the blade and lost a testicle I understand, for which I have regrets. But Trump got off lightly, losing only half a leg. I'll get the ginger cunt next time" he concluded.

When asked by a reporter from CNN if he had any regrets, Archie replied: "Only that I didn't get the bastard's cock and balls" before gulping on a can of Irn-Bru, who's manufacturer Barr's, now manage the affairs of Archie and his family.

When asked about how Archie managed to get onto the course, greenkeeper Angus McPherson-McFlurrie. told Fox News: "Och noo, you know how these fences are, you think you've locked them and then you realise, you got distracted and must have left the bastard open. Aw well, these things happen."

Local landlord of the Pheasant Inn, Jock McSporran, told CNN: "That Trump chappie, he's ruffled a few feathers in these parts, what with buying out the golf club, the football club, and the local scout hut. There's a few out there who'd like to give him a piece of their mind" he told the reporter, whilst chewing on a fried Mars Bar.

There's further reports of UFO sightings over various football stadiums in the UK. Family of the owners of Newcastle United and Cardiff City disappear, only to be found 48 hours later, with no memory of where they've been, except for, under hypnosis, images of alien like creatures, dressed in football kits, asking them questions about 'financial fair play.'

Gary Lineker is appointed UN Secretary of State after some wonderful mediation work after a dispute over cuttlefish and squid fishing between Iceland and Norway, the usually chilled out Nordic fishermen, becoming uncharacteristically combative over the perceived straying of the other into disputed territorial waters.

Israel and Palestine are next on the list of issues to be sorted by the mild-mannered crisp connoisseur.

Greta Thunberg successfully proves the DNA on the burger revealed by Murdoch's News Corporation was not hers and 'planted' by the disgraced broadcaster, Piers Morgan, who now heads up the organization.

The attempt to disgrace the environmentalist came about after she had exposed and thwarted the attempt to build a golf and casino complex in Greenland by a joint venture between News Corporation and Donald

Trump.

Jet skis are banned around the island of Anglesey after extensive lobbying by Bear Grylls. Jim Smith from Jet Set Willy, a jet ski business recently set up by the Manchester based entrepreneur and suspected drug dealer, claims this is anti-English discrimination.

Bear, swimming in Holyhead harbour at the time, responded to reporters saying: "it's nothing to do with where you're from, it's more the noisy, inconsiderate, ecologically bereft, selfish, people who think they could do what they want in our oceans who are the discriminators. Fuck off Jet Set Willy and take your gas guzzling glorified pedalos with you."

Cayman Islands and other tax havens are compulsorily taken over by the UN under new international treaty 'The Making the World a Fairer Place Treaty 2024.'

As part of the deal, funds in the various offshore accounts are confiscated and allocated to poorer countries and good causes.

A new international facility for convicted high profile individuals, such as TV presenters, actors, politicians, being housed there on an island template originally designed by the architect for Alcatraz.

Cutting the ribbon for the opening is Boris Johnson who promptly after the ceremony takes his place as the inaugural inmate, alongside other politicians Rishi Sunak, Jacob Rees-Mogg, Suella Braverman and Matt Hancock.

"I'm proud to be the first guest" is all the disgraced former British prime minister says as he's led away from the paparazzi.

Situated on marshland between two rocky peninsulas, creating a natural moat, inhabited by an indigenous ecosystem supporting an array of predatory wildlife, the purpose-built building is state of the art.

Chris Packham and Michaela Strachan, filming a live feed documentary, for Channel 4, inadvertently catch on camera the moment the floppy haired former privileged arse-wipe, makes a run for freedom to a nearby dinghy seized by buddy Rishi Sunak from migrants crossing the English Channel.

Misjudging the slope of the sandbank he'd jumped upon, Mr Johnson hurtled into a deep lagoon and into the open jaws of a grateful cayman. The irony that the islands where he and his cronies had previously kept their ill-gotten funds, was now the cause of his demise, was not lost on the Channel 4 audience, who were, as grateful as the chomping cayman for the producer keeping the live stream going, despite tv guidelines over such gruesome scenarios.

The others who had made it to the dinghy were eaten slowly by sharks and piranha's who appeared to enjoy taking their time devouring these human plankton.

In Rwanda, the last of the extradited migrants, on their way back to the UK for a new life, couldn't help but grin as they watched the scene play out live on the tv sets on their flight home.

Nurse Kearns says "turn off" to the Big TV and obediently the footage disappears into a dot. We play Countdown and I get the numbers, three nine letter words and outscore both players, although I do miss out on the conundrum which is 'snowboard' which is a fucking tough one to be fair. Rachel Riley looks like she might be pregnant again. I feel a yearning for Carol Vorderman and wonder what she's doing now.

The presenter has some banter with some female comedian who's just come out as being manically depressed, but she looks happy today as she recounts an anecdote involving Anthony Hopkins and some former footballer who went for a night out in the west end of London only to wake up in a Rhyl nightclub without any memory of how they got there.

I remember a friend who used to watch Countdown on Channel 4 Plus 1 and then played his daft mate for money and who never questioned why he always got the conundrum.

I do a 10 km run which almost kills me, but I don't engage in any conversation with the physio who tells me something about his wife and a PHD in something to do with philosophy and an awards ceremony in the Philippines.

I nod when it feels right and then I shower and then we watch a drama from Norway which involves a serial killer, a female detective who sleeps around, lots of drone shots of forests and lakes and glaciers and a local weirdo who everyone thinks is the killer, when it is in fact, the local priest.

I ask if I can have a glass of wine to go with my meds. They say no. I ask if I can have a Tizer. They say it doesn't exist anymore. I suggest a glass of Sunny Delight; they shake their heads, saying it was banned as it was like drinking a glass of nuclear war.

I go to bed. It takes a while to get to sleep. The sky is heavy, lead black, no stars, that dead-end time of night when it can feel like the weight of the world hangs heavy on your head and the anchovy of the day becomes the dark, heavy blue whale of the night.

Day 8, 2030

I tell Dr Paskin that I really don't want to talk about my dreams. I mention they were hardcore: Violence, sex, murder, it had it all. She says she's got a tough skin and she needs to hear this and it's part of the recovery process. I look at her and shake my head. You asked for it. Ok here goes.

'I'm on an airplane with a group of animals, the majority of which can talk. The pigs seem to be important in this social structure with a gorilla in overall charge. I'm essentially an air hostess serving them tumblers of brandy and port. They become more and more raucous as they become intoxicated. They start to become inappropriate and despite an appeal by the captain, they became an unmanageable rabble. The pigs are disgusting, slobbering all over me, the hippos aren't much better, the gorilla sets no type of example and if anything, encourages the despicable behaviour. I wake as the animals collectively begin to engulf me, the noise a cacophony of squeals and grunts, an altogether sound of horror.'

Dr Paskin agrees that this sounds unpleasant, and she can understand the panic and the fear. I also mention again the dream of being at Wembley Stadium and Brett Ormerod missing a sitter against Newport County and a man in a purple sweater giving me a wanker sign at the final whistle.

My gym instructor today is Mike Muldoon for which I'm grateful, as Steve Massey-Ferguson really loves the burpee and has it seems, devised every type of variant to it, such as, dumbbell curl burpees, a shoulder press burpee, a reverse plank burpee, a handstand burpee, and back flip burpee. It's absurd. Mike is much more old school and loves the hill sprints and the rows and some basic floor work with sit ups, press ups and the ropes, which is my favourite.

We spent the rest of the morning watching quiz shows: Blockbusters, 15-1, Countdown. I remember them all. I went on Blockbuster as a kid I tell Nurse Kearns. Can I have a 'P' please Bob. I howl with laughter. Nurse Kearns is too young to remember Bob Holness and the acute comedy a contestant would indulge in if they chose the 'P' segment on the board they had to navigate to win the game and extraordinarily meagre prizes. Who Wants to Be a Millionaire, this was not.

I got all the questions correct. We played some archived episodes of Countdown. I do the conundrums which even the studio audience can't. I get the numbers that Carol Vorderman is left scratching her genius head over. I recall that Carol is from my hometown of Prestatyn.

We then played Bullseye and a couple from Wolverhampton won a speed boat. On another episode, the winners turn down the gamble, saying 'they've had a lovely day,' and 'we'll let the others have a chance at the jackpot.'

The others also pass, with the third couple choosing to retain the £15 and a Bouncy Bully that they're now the proud owners of. From beyond the stage curtains, host, Jim Bowen, reveals 'look at what you could have won' – a de-lux caravan, always a de-lux fucking caravan.

Dr Paskin directs the Big TV to turn off and this is where they finally put me in front of the mirror, to let me see how far I've decayed over this decade.

When Dr Paskin sat down with me that morning as I drank my coffee, she might have said something about this being a large step and if it's too much I just have to say and it's all about doing what feels right. I'd nod of course as I have an embedded desire to be friendly, to be nice, to please people. This is what my psychometrics have revealed. I used to think this was a positive personality trait. Now I'm not so sure. Being nice can possibly be a weakness, a negative; some people take advantage of your niceness.

"So, are you ready?"

"Fuck, I'm not sure."

It's like I've been going on about it since my time here and now I'm terrified. She says it's up to me, there's a mirror we've put in the bathroom, a full-length effort so you can view the entirety of yourself. It's that anticipation thing again. Deferred gratification. The act is never better than the thought before it.

I think hard. I swallow deep, take in a whole load of air. I stare blankly towards the Big TV, that despite it being off, has an image of a goldfish bowl on it. This is what happens when my fascination gets the better of me. My impulse control is not what it could be. I'm a bit embarrassed disclosing this but it's an essential part of the story. I open my eyes and stare at this reflection, this image of me, something I haven't seen for ten long years.

So here goes, there are a few oddities that you really can't pass over when I stand here, looking back at myself:

I have a full-blown beard (I look like a Nordic cross-country skier), a tattoo of the crest of Wrexham Football Club on my left calf, there is of course, the elephant in the corner that is my abnormally sized penis.

Dr Paskin asks if this triggers anything. It's been ten years, near enough. If you remember anything about your former self, pre-coma, this might be something of a shock. You've lost weight, a lot of weight. You've aged. It's a natural process. Are you recognising anything?

It's insane right, I wake from a decade long coma and can't remember who I am, but I can speak fluent Norwegian, Icelandic, Russian, possibly more and have a knowledge of facts that make me answer every quiz show question together with abstract knowledge of stuff linked to Wrexham F.C.

The reflection is something completely alien to me. It's a stranger. An imposter. A third party staring back at me. My instant reaction is that, and this sounds boastful, but that he's quite handsome, rugged looking; he's friendly, has strange eyes, green grey in colour, eyes that slant at the edges.

I don't recognise him. I don't recognise me I should say. And I know it's me as I look at this, but I don't recognise it. Not one bit. It's a weird feeling. I find myself touching part of my face, my body, to check that the corresponding movement is reflected at me, to double check it is me being reflected. It's fucking strange.

It'll take time, says Dr Paskin.

Don't rush it.

She noticed I don't recognise myself and I think she knows this, it's big news to me, a massive reaction. It's something she didn't expect is how I perceive her facial expression. I think she's waited for this time. And now I've failed her, disappointed her. She thought I was ready, and I wasn't. Putting it quite simply, I haven't got a Scooby Doo who this fucker is. I can speak loads of languages, I can remember random fragments of football matches, I'm amazing at quiz shows, but I don't recognise a reflection of myself. Fuck me.

There's nothing more to really say, so Dr Paskin tells the Big TV to 'Play.'

2027

Iconic pop star Madonna is rumoured to be in talks with Prestatyn Town F.C., the interest linked to an episode of Crackerjack she watched back in the 1980s when madcap host Stuey Francis, of 'I'm so excited I could crush a grape' fame, trod on a top hat and said, where's this place and the Krankies, the Scottish comedy duo, replied Press Me Hat In, a clear play on words of the seaside town.

Madonna, touring her Like a Virgin album at the time, watching the show from her tour bus, thought this was hilarious and when she noticed Ryan Reynolds talking about the club he now owned, remembered Prestatyn and Wales, and decided this was the one for her.

Chairman, Tony Apple is quoted in the local newspaper, the Rhyl and Prestatyn Visitor as saying: "Yeah, I'm more of a Killing Joke, New Model Army, The Damned, kind of listener but yeah, you can't help but hum along to some of her tunes, and that video with the Black Christ, was pretty revolutionary at the time and who doesn't like a bit of writhing lingerie on a Venetian gondola."

F.C. Romans of Chester City (2024) announce a new sponsorship deal with Danish block experts, Lego with their Bumpers Lane ground now officially known as The Lego Ground. Danny DeVito, shopping for his morning bagel in Manhattan, is spotted wearing a T-shirt which has a chunk of Lego on it and the slogan: 'shit ground, no fans.'

Donald Trump has an assassination free year and is spotted having lunch with Elon Musk and Wham Bam Bum, fueling rumours of some kind of looming collaboration.

Day 9, 2030

I wake to the sound of birdsong, the dawn chorus providing a serene soundtrack to a beautiful morning, the sun low and white, throwing out shadows that dance across the room. I've slept soundly and eaten a breakfast that is quite spectacular: berries, smoothies, croissants, and there's a vibrancy to my tastebuds that is difficult to articulate.

I tell Dr Paskin about a sequence of dreams, interconnected, involving the hammerhead shark people, wearing suits and bowler hats, provocative jellyfish, trying to get me into a nightclub but which is probably a whorehouse, called Stingrays. She asks me if there was anything sexual about the dream. I told her I cuddled up to a beautiful turquoise seahorse but there was no penetration.

Dr Paskin directs me towards the Big TV: footage of a graduation - this is you she says. A law degree. Liverpool 1994. The man presenting went on to preside over the Hillsborough Disaster - remember that?

Next, a birth scene, a glob of baby being placed on the chest of a woman who looks knackered but insanely happy. There's a presumption of a long birth, the midwife, the woman who has given birth, the man, standing next to the bed doing something with a mobile phone that is laughably outdated, tech from another generation.

Then some footage of me, looking younger than I am now, next to me a young child, at a football match, some background noise, a child manically waving a flag. I'm drinking what looks like coffee from a Styrofoam cup, the child drinking from a container that looks like it has Spider-Man on its side.

Dr Paskin, Nurse Bennett, and Dr Ferguson play The Chase, an ITV game show hosted by Bradley Walsh. I remember playing this in my former life, but I don't think I ever got that much right. Now, I'm getting everything. I know absolutely everything.

I know things about music, art, science, literature, everything. We play Mastermind, hosted by some robot called Magnus Robotson. I answer all the questions on the specialist subjects and general knowledge.

We watched some news footage. They tell me to buzz again if I recognise anything: A man with absurd yellow hair is stood in a stadium. There're thousands of people wearing baseball jackets, shouting over and over: 'We love Trump'. I buzz. I recognise this buffoon.

A posh English politician standing outside 10 Downing Street. I buzz. I recognise this man. He's wearing a face mask. The paparazzi assembled along the street are wearing face masks. On the podium it says Keep your distance, save the NHS, save lives.

I buzz. I buzz. I keep on buzzing.

Dr Paskin might be saying: these are all the things that happened in the months leading to the accident. The 2020s was a strange decade. She's saying stuff but all I'm seeing is her mouth, fish like, her lips moving but there's nothing coming out but the sound of static that you might hear when the television went off and the national anthem would play out and the screen would fade away into a dot that would linger for a while, before leaving the room empty and blank.

She directs gently the Big TV to 'Play memories.'

A series of photographs, footage, appears:

A baby outside a hospital.

A baby on a beach with another child slightly older.

A film - a superhero. Looks like Spider-Man but isn't Spider-Man. Violent yet funny. Quips about stacking a dishwasher whilst decapitating a bad guy. This is seriously fucking funny.

People queuing outside a low flat building.

Buzz buzz buzz.

I remember this. Are these memories? Are these my memories?

A football match, some massive floodlights standing like alien spaceships from a sci-fi movie throwing silver light onto lush turf.

"Do you recognise them? Do you recognise these scenes? This is a very important part of the healing process."

"No, I don't recognise anything", I say.

On the screen there is a picture of a mangled car. It is difficult to make out what type of car it is. It looks black, perhaps a Mercedes or a Volkswagen. A line of policeman, fireman, people wearing luminous yellow and orange jackets. They look like they are assessing, discussing; a feeling of desperate terror coming from the shot.

Do you recognise this scene she says?

I stare into the television screen and blink hard. I take a drink from the tumbler of water which she has placed beside me on the side table. I hold the water in my mouth for maybe five or six seconds and then swallow it in seven tiny gulps. I can feel her looking for a reaction, trying not to be too obvious but I can feel the stare, peripherally and her waiting for me to recognise something.

This means nothing to me I say. Absolutely nothing. It's a complete blank. Blankety, Blank I add, for some reason. That's fine. Remember none of these are trick questions. Please just say what you feel.

There's a crack on the window and a gust that picks up and makes us both look towards the grey sky outside, a V of geese migrating somewhere away from here, the leader now taking his place at the back having a well-earned rest as the peloton forever revolving, efficiently journeying halfway around the globe.

There's a blast of hailstones, rebounding off the window, the building, a thud of thunder, a flash bulb of lightning. I love a storm, its energy, the sheer enormity of its power and force. It makes you feel so insignificant, a speck of shit, a grain of sand, a microbe in the deepest darkest ocean, a microscopic octopus, shapeshifting, ink-blasting, invisible in the scheme of nature.

I look towards a gap in the skirting board which I first noticed when I woke up. I imagine a Tom & Jerry cartoon world going on behind the wall, a cartoon world where everything is fine, a strip of blue sky, an inch high, a yellow sun with a hat and vintage Ray-bans.

Dr Paskin tells me they have a surprise for me. Tomorrow. It's massive, she says, her beautiful eyes widening, pupils dilating. I need to expect that it might be something of a shock. The reaction, she's pre-empting is completely natural. It's going to be something of a head-fuck. That's what she says, how she frames it, 'head-fuck.'

I admit it, and it's probably wrong and exposes some weakness within me, from my past and maybe I'm slightly deviant but if I'm being completely honest with you, I find it sexy, this kind of language.

Dr Paskin, oblivious thankfully to my inner thoughts, directs the Big TV: 'Play 2028' and the Big TV blinks into devastating action.

Donald Trump announces he's taken over Scottish football team, Cowdenbeath United and has applied for them to play in the MLS where they will now be based. Their ground, The Donald Trump Arena is to be transformed into a state-of-the-art Golfing and Leisure Complex.

After extensive lobbying by Joe Wicks and Bear Grylls, new legislation is introduced creating new tax incentives for those hitting 100,000 Steps a week. To avoid the possibility of fraud, a new computer chip is to be inserted into every member of the population at the same time as they have their annual Covid vaccination.

Wales are up to 6th in the world rankings after a 5-0 victory over England at an ecstatic Racecourse Ground, Wrexham with local starlet Dewi Jones coming on from the bench to bag a brace, the ageing English defence unable to handle the vibrancy and verve of the young Welsh side.

Bear Grylls becomes Secretary of State for Education and introduces rock climbing, sea-kayaking, and bug-eating into the mainstream curriculum.

Man United, Chelsea and Tottenham join a breakaway league with F.C. Shanghai, Melbourne A.F.C., A.C. Milan, Real Madrid, and L.A. Galaxy.

Manchester City and Liverpool say they wouldn't have joined even if they were asked. Championship Clubs weren't eligible responds Michel Platini, Chairman of the new Donald Trump International League of Soccer-ball.

Liverpool is relegated to the third tier of English football in a final game injury time defeat to Forest Green Rovers. Manager Jurgen Klopp, spectacle-less after pioneering laser treatment, resigns after the game and immediately joins Marrakesh United who are invited to the new international league after the USA and Morocco sign a historic trade deal following the discovery of vast new oil fields in the Moroccan desert.

Elon Musk announces he will be going to Mars. His co-astronaut will be announced next year. It's going to be "out of this world" he announces.

Terrible fires scorch Australia and New Zealand.

Wrexham Football Club are promoted to League 1 after beating Sheffield Wednesday in a play-off final. Retro Wrexham Mascot, Rockin' Robin, brought back after a 20,000 strong petition was presented to club owners, has a fist fight with counterpart, Ollie Owl, the two being arrested in a brawl that spilled over after Ollie allegedly called Rockin' a 'sheep shagger.'

The club decides to revert to Wrex the Dragon and to retire Rockin' Robin for the foreseeable future, whilst the dust settles.

The campaign for Welsh independence gathers pace with the term 'sheep shagger' officially recognised as a 'hate crime.'

Donald Trump loses his other leg in a freak lift accident in his New York home at Trump Towers. Reports of a man in a kilt drinking from a bottle of whiskey being seen 'hanging around' the basement of the building have yet to be substantiated.

Trump appears bullish in a hospital bed and clarifies after rumours he is now only comprised of a head and a torso, that he does also have a left arm, albeit from the elbow up, and that his buddy Elon was close to finalising a prosthetic robot body that would restore Trump to his former glory with some 'added turbo power.'

Joe Wicks brings out a new range of athletic socks called 'Joe Wicks Athletic Socks.'

Hugh Jackman challenges Ryan Reynolds to a boxing match to be held in the amphitheatre in Chester. Russell Crowe is rumoured to be the referee if the bout can be arranged.

Wrexham F.C. reached the semi-finals of the FA Cup, losing to Chesterfield with the winning goal coming from an intercepted back-pass. They do manage to win the Johnstone Paints Trophy, a reserve team coming through to beat Liverpool in the final.

Day 10, 2030

A series of dreams is how I explain it to Dr Paskin. The hammerhead shark people were there but then there was a meteor that struck America and Elon Musk and Donald Trump lifted off in a rocket and went to live in a commune that had secretly been built on the far side of the moon.

A new trainer, Ifor Williams, puts me through my paces. He smells of manure and silage, but he sets up a circuit session which includes a lot of rope and abdomen work and to be fair, lays off the burpees and the mountain climbers which I've grown to detest.

We have a leisurely day watching videos of football matches I've attended involving Wrexham and Wales and there's a particular highlight when a player called Hal Robson-Kanu does a sublime turn against Belgium, helping Wales reach the semi-finals in France, 2016. I remember this and the Don't Take Me Home songs that drifted through the French streets that glorious summer.

There was also some footage of England losing to Iceland and the former manager Steve Maclaren commentating on the game, summarising that everything was under control and England were looking decent. And then you see his face contort on the myriad of TV screens that fill the wall of the studio, as Iceland score to win the game.

We play Countdown and Dr Paskin smashes the conundrums and then we watch some videos of me playing with small children on a beach and then watching a football match in a stadium somewhere.

I ask for a Nutty Bar but Nurse Kearns says they were discontinued some years ago and the nearest thing to it is perhaps a Picnic but I decline as I was never a fan of the raisin involvement so instead, I opt for a Turkish Delight by Fry's (beware of awful imitations) and cut this into four sections with a knife and then eat the chocolate coating before allow the pink inners to gently melt on my tongue.

I asked Nurse Kearns for her Top 5 Confectionary. She goes for:

1. Chunky Kit Kat.
2. Boost.
3. Mars.
4. Twix.
5. Tunnocks Teacakes.

(This somehow, evoking some memory of a game against St Mirren Reserves).

Dr Paskin goes for:

1. Marks & Spencer's chocolate rings.
2. Chocolate Hobnobs.
3. Double Decker.
4. Jammy Dodgers.
5. Jaffa Cakes.

We spend the rest of the afternoon having the old 'is a Jaffa cake a cake or a biscuit' debate. We can't reach a consensus and to break the deadlock, Dr Paskin turns to the Big TV and says 'Play.'

Um Bongo is relaunched by Donald Trump.

Wembley Stadium is hit by a commercial airliner flying into London from Afghanistan.

Joe Wicks announces a range of white goods kitchen equipment under the brand 'Joe Wicks Kitchen Equipment.'

F.C. Romans of Chester City (2024) are promoted to League 1.

Madonna's takeover of Prestatyn F.C. appears to have hit a snag with one of the Committee XX XXXXXXXX (name retracted for legal reasons) stating that: "She wasn't really the face of the brand that we are trying to promote here in Prestatyn, us being a keen hub of the community. I mean, she'd perhaps be a bit better suited for our neighbours at Rhyl F.C. or perhaps Holyhead Hotspurs."

Tony Apple resigns and sets up a U2 tribute band called Me3.

A Big Cat is sighted outside the ground of Chester F.C.

Ian Rush tells reporters: "It looked like a small horse, but it also looked like a large cat, but thinking on, it did make a neighing sound and was eating a carrot so was probably a horse, albeit quite a cat looking horse."

Prince Andrew is convicted of various sex offences and is sentenced to 20 years house arrest. Ex wife, Sarah Ferguson says: "Randy bastard got what he deserved."

Aled Jones, young left winger for Wrexham F.C., announces he is gay, leading to several players 'coming out.'

Day 11, 2030

I wake to the sound of glorious birdsong and sit for a while, watching the sky transcend from a pale pink through to orange and then a crimson red. A plane hurtles through, there's some traffic noise as the commuter's inch forward in their daily gridlock, listening to tunes and podcasts telling them how to live a fulfilling life.

Dr Paskin and Dr Mills entered my room, and we exchanged pleasantries and Dr Mills says that I'm doing well and am recovering quicker than anybody expected. I tell them both about my dream of being a human in a cartoon underwater environment and there were cartoon rays, lobsters, giant octopus spraying ink all over the place and then a strange looking creature known as a yeti crab that blindly kept banging into my legs.

I'm then playing a football match with these sea-creatures, and we're all dressed in a Wrexham kit with TikTok written across the front and I've no idea what TikTok is, but I noticed it on some footage that was playing on the Big TV the other day.

I do a 10k treadmill run with Mike Muldoon and then shower and spend the afternoon watching clips of football matches from the weekend.

Dr Paskin says it's time for the Big TV and directs it to 'Play.'

Joe Wicks is elected Prime Minister with his new Health and Well-Being Party holding an overwhelming majority, with the Conservatives only holding on to a few seats in the Home Counties with New Labour coming in second.

Plaid Cymru dominates the Welsh seats and there's a feeling that independence might not be far away. There's still no Monarch in place with nobody wanting to take on the position. It seems the UK might sleepwalk into being a Republic.

One of the new Prime Minister's changes is to introduce HIIT sessions in the chamber before every sitting. The Prime Minister's questions are often now taken whilst wearing his Wrexham F.C. tracksuit.

He moves quickly to appoint Bear Grylls as his No 2. Bear carries out a press conference whilst abseiling down Kodak 2, in the Andes, after a lucrative sponsorship package is announced.

Michael Sheen is announced as the new First Minister for Wales, his impassioned speeches becoming a rousing anthem for proponents of Welsh Nationalism.

Richard Branson is in talks with local Sherpas to sponsor the Himalayas.

Elon Musk becomes the first civilian to land on the Moon and is quick to sponsor the sphere which is now known as Elon's Moon. His co-astronaut is Donald Trump who, on a live stream, drinking from a can of Um Bongo, declares: Um Bongo Um Bongo, it's out of this World-O.

Joe Wicks announces any citizen not hitting 70,000 steps a week will not be entitled to social security (with certain exceptions for people with defined disabilities). Those hitting over 70,000 will receive fitness payments tiered on a staggered scale. Anyone hitting 100,000 every week over a period of 12 months will receive a bonus £10,000 fitness pay-out.

Donald Trump survives another assassination attempt whilst out playing golf in his new robotic suit, in Bull Bay, Anglesey, where he is rumoured to be considering buying local club F.C. Cemaes Bay.

Locals, unhappy with any form of outsider coming onto the island to pilfer its assets, plant a crude and rudimentary incendiary device under their golf cart which explodes on the Par 3, 10th hole, with a gentle thud.

Unscathed but for a double bogey 5, Trump says, "this will not put me off this wonderful peninsula of England and I've always loved Tom Jones and Shirley Bassey and that Dylan Thomas bloke. I also love that 69 Guns song by Welsh rockers The Alarm, I think they're called."

Speaking exclusively to the Anglesey Free Press, he continued: "Wrexham F.C. are one of the better English sides, now those American blokes own them. I quite fancy buying a club in Wales. It looks like the place to be, reminds me a bit of Alaska but with way more sheep and daffodils."

Deadpool 10 is released to rave reviews, the World Premier held at the Wrexham Odeon, with the squad of Wrexham F.C. who feature heavily in the movie, enjoying their night out on the Red Carpet, all wearing a clothing range, designed by striker, Ollie Palmer.

Freemasonry is officially classified by the new government as an unlawful organization, viewed in the same light as right-wing groups like the National Front.

Wicks announces: "if anyone approaches you by offering a 'funny' handshake, report the corrupt fucker immediately to the authorities."

Several high-ranking police officials and civil servants are arrested and charged with corruption and conspiracy charges.

Donald Trump dies whilst training for his trip to Mars.

After a series of alien abductions affecting the families of foreign owned football clubs, several overseas owners gift their clubs to local business and fan-owned consortiums. A salary and branding cap is agreed by the government so that footballers will earn a wage no more than that of a high-ranking civil servant.

In a house in Wrexham, Dewi Jones, is contacted via Facetime by an alien called A.L.F. who wants to know more about humans, and intrigued by the Disney Documentary, Welcome to Wrexham, thought it would be a good idea to contact a Wrexham supporter.

Dewi passes the information on to the authorities, with Gary Lineker, appointed to be the ambassador to planet earth with discussions between the alien race and humanity with a view to a collaboration over various issues including technology, health, social structures, peace, and setting up an intergalactic football league.

Day 12, 2030

Despite the beautiful pink sky and low summer sun, I've woken in tears, my chest rising uncontrollably, my breathing out of control. I feel I'm having a cardiac arrest. I've had the worst nightmare. I won't bore you with it as other people's nightmares are such a drag. But let me just say it was a horror show. If you could capture it as a movie, it would be the best horror film ever.

I tell Dr Paskin in a hushed voice. I tell her every detail. It was in monochrome, a strange award-winning horror, dream-noir: Twins Peaks crashes into Psycho. Dr Paskin starts to cry. Nurse Kearns enters the room and instantly starts to blub. In terms of the flowing of raw emotion, it's absolute carnage.

My Crocs are damp from the flow of my tears. The versatile footwear at least allows the liquid to spread across my foot, something a brogue or a trainer simply wouldn't be able to deal with.

Crocs aren't given the respect they deserve. They're versatile and light and airy and apart from the plastic and the environmental impact, they're truly wonderful footwear. All it will take is a celebrity endorsement, a superhero taking them on as its footwear of choice and they'll become super-cool, just you see.

I do a gym session, a fifteen-minute sprint they do in the special forces, and you must go as far as you can in that time. I did 4.1km. I'm fucking wrecked but buzzing; the wonderful paradox that extreme exercise brings.

I tell Physio Steel to throw everything he's got at me, burpees, mountain climbers, speed rowing, goblet squats, static lunges, come on, beast me you absolute twat and I'm finding myself shouting, 'beast me, beast me' which is probably wrong on so many fronts.

We then move on to throwing a medicine ball above my head and throwing it down, heaving some dumb bells from a squat into a curl into a shoulder press.

I love the feeling of post exercise, the endorphins racing around my body. I shower and submerge myself in the ultra-powerful multi jet shower that throws steaming jets of water from all angles to my head, my back, right up my arse (which is surprisingly pleasant), if I position it strategically. Shower technology really has come on. I stand and let the water soak me, submerged in soap bubbles that come out of a slot with a verbal command. I write a series of letters in the condensation. My name?

I direct Alexa to play me some Icelandic alternative rock and some Sigur Ros blasts through the speakers that appear as air vents in the corners of the room. Then some soothing Bon Iver. Then some A-HA and I think I'm heterosexual, but that Morten Harket is a handsome fucker.

I yell at Alexa to tell me what the weather is like in Laos: 42 degrees she responds with humidity of 32.5%.

Then, feeling like I'm on a roll, I fire some deeper shit at her:

Who am I?

What is my name?

Why am I here?

What's the capital of Belarus?

What is the average size of a 50-year-old man's penis?

Are all polar bears left-handed?

Is it cool to wear Crocs?

She says 'I do not have that information' to all these requests, apart from the capital of Belarus, which is Minsk if you're interested.

I say, 'fuck you Alexa, thanks for nothing.'

I recall the nightmare, and cry again and once I've settled down and my breathing is back in check and the tears have stopped exploding, my attention turns to these medical warriors who must have seen some shit in their lives. For them to be so affected really bothers me. However, whilst I appreciate this must be tough for these angels, for now, I need to look out for myself. Let's be fair, I've also had a tough time and some fucker really needs to explain a few things, fill me in on how it is I'm here in this place.

Dr Paskin tells me to sit down whilst pouring me a coffee, directing me with a tilt of her beautiful head to look at the Big TV.

"This might help" she says, "this might give you some closure."

"Hallelujah, praise the fucking lord" I declare.

Some footage plays out on the Big TV.

Ryan Reynolds narrates over the images.

'It's 2021.

So, how did we end up here?

I'd say, there are various possibilities:

You got attacked by a group of football hooligans fueled by anti-Welsh sentiment?

A Hungarian man knocked you out at five a side football, incorrectly thinking you were being anti-Hungarian?

You were on your way to a meeting. You were involved in a car accident and your car collided with a car driven by actors, myself, Ryan Reynolds, and my buddy, the one with the hard to pronounce name, Rob McElhenney. You were part of the legal team dealing with the sale of the club from the Supporters Trust to Rob and myself. You assisted the club with legal matters for several years, alongside Spencer Harris. You've been in a coma for nearly 10 years?

It's got to be one of the above; we've narrowed it down to try and make some sense out of this sorry shitstorm.

We've been playing a series of events from your life to see if they trigger any memories, or 'memory blasts' as the experts call it. You've remembered some weird shit and that thing with the languages and your big dick and the general knowledge, that's weird right, but apparently it does, by all accounts, happen.

There was once a woman from Armenia who woke up from a 5-year coma, speaking fluent Welsh and was orchestra-proficient in playing the harp.'

He says these things as if he were reading out a shopping list: broccoli, bread, salt fish, bagels, tampons. These are the things that've been playing out over the Big TV, piecing together fragments of my shattered past as if I were a broken doll being put back together. It's been a journey buddy, but you've come through better than anyone expected.

Ryan finishes his monologue on the Big TV saying, on an endless loop: Don't rush things, the brain really is an amazing thing, you have powers of recovery you would never have imagined.

In my head, behind the walls, a cartoon plays out with animated mice chasing animated cats, their heads blasted apart by animated hand grenades, exploding up animated backsides, an animated world sometimes feeling more appealing than the real thing.

Dr Paskin says tomorrow is going to be a big day, a pivotal stage in your life, in your recovery; it will be a lot to take in. Dr Mills hands me my meds and an ice-cold drink of 7 Up. It's a tasty beverage, not too fizzy, with a hint of lemon and lime. I gulp this concoction down and fall into a heavy sleep which is entwined with hallucinations, segments of images that may or may not have happened in real life, pre-coma.

Day 13, 2030

When I wake, after a quick breakfast, we skip the dream analysis, the gym, the game shows, the video memories, and the whole place is busier than I ever can remember. Everyone is here, all the physios, the doctors, the porters, the nurses – everyone is buzzing.

On the Big TV, images of football matches playing out, an Ollie Kearns header, an injury time winner, a Paul Mullin overhead kick, images from It's Always Sunny in Philadelphia, scenes from the pandemic, various clips from Deadpool. Dr Paskin enters the room, and everything falls deathly quiet.

"Your visitors have arrived" she announces.

"Fuck" I respond. It's far from eloquent but it's all I can come out with; all I can process. My head is a kaleidoscope of emotion, of fears and hopes and dreams and dread and pondering the question of who the fuck is visiting me and fundamentally will this enhance or detract my absurd, abstract existence.

The visitors sign in by retina recognition followed by fingerprint scanning and they're offered coffee or fruit capsules in the reception pod, a window-less room with inspirational quotes on walls from inspirational people in society: YouTuber's, rappers, footballers, influencers:

Believe in yourself Hun.

Don't give a flying fuck about anyone else bitch.

You're the sunrise, you're the sunset, you're my heartbeat.

The motivation these slogans creates is underwhelming to me but perhaps it enhances the hopes and lives of others and in any event, it fills the walls and eats away at time as these people wait to see the patients, these fruit-loops, space cadets, loony tunes in our pale grey outfits, like we should be fixing tyre tubes in a factory for aircraft.

On checking my enormous watch, I'm anxious that I've only achieved 7,452 steps. If I don't make 10,000, I won't be entitled to my evening snack. Reward and achievement. That's what it's all about.

Dr Paskin, sitting in a futuristic chair looking more made-up than usual, urges me to sit in a chair next to her, the same design but in a darker shade of off-white. There's a shift of colour, in tone, in sound. It could be the medication; it could be that a man has entered the room dressed head to toe in red Lycra, taking a seat directly opposite us both.

The silence feels like it lingers for a millennium but, is only probably five or six seconds. Dr Paskin shuffles in her seat before half smiling, twisting a finger in her hair. If she were so inclined, she would be introducing me now to this superhero. But she seems to want to hoard him for herself. I mean, this should be all about me, right? Come on, where's your professionalism Dr Paskin.

There's a poster of Deadpool 10 in between the door and the window. It's the image I've seen on the Big TV, the various clips from the movie. She seems somewhat starstruck. There's an energy in the room. This was supposed to be about me. It's all about me.

"I should introduce myself," says the man dressed from head to toe in the red skin-tight suit, "I'm Deadpool."

The superhero says first and foremost, he's sorry for the inconvenience, for the accident caused. It really was quite freakish, like something out of a movie. I came out of nowhere, a side-street and yes, I should have seen you, but I didn't and look what happened, in that half-second.

"It shows you the fragility of our existence" says the other guy, a bloke with a beard, strange accent, probably small-town America.

"And hey, thank fuck we didn't kill you" says Deadpool.

The other guy says, "yeah that's so true."

"Fuck" says Deadpool, "that could have been a whole different kettle of shit-fish."

"Hell, you said it Deadpool. A coma in the overall scheme of things isn't that bad. I mean, you got to get a ten-year nap after all."

The other bloke high fives Deadpool and blows out his cheeks adding "and it's a right bonus having that big dick right, that's a real win."

"And the languages and being great at game shows" adds Deadpool.

"By the way," the other guy says, "I'm Rob. I'm, well, the other guy, the one with the hard to pronounce name."

Dr Paskin guffaws. It's hardly side-splitting stuff but she's laughing like her life depends on it, as if the cast of Monty Python have come in and performed their greatest hits, whilst tripping on acid. The room falls silent. If you were here, I'd guess you'd notice the tangible awkwardness.

"Oh, my fuck" says Deadpool, breaking the silence, looking down to my feet.

"Fuck," he's wearing Crocs, Ryan," the other guy says to Deadpool.

Deadpool follows his stare.

"OMG, it's way worse than that" he says, "they're only fucking camouflage Crocs would you believe."

"What we have here," he whispers, all melodramatic, sexy superhero style "is what is commonly known as in the trade, as a…"

Rob, the other guy, shouts out:

"CROC WANKER."

And they howl uncontrollably like they've just invented the very notion of comedy itself. I smile, looking for something else to focus on, starlings on a wire through the window, a line of traffic, some cloud formation over distant hills, but it's all blank. I can't make out anything, just a void, a white milky transparent oblong of emptiness as there's no fucking window in here.

He says it was that adjustment thing with the other side of the road, coupled with the jet lag. It really is underrated he offers to the room, to the camera, to me and Dr Paskin. I've tried everything, no alcohol, sleep adjustment to the new time zone, underripe bananas, watching Deadpool 2 on repeat, but nothing ever touches it. It's a type of torture. It really fucks with your system.

Dr Paskin interjects and reaffirms; the effects of jet lag really are underestimated and there needs to be more respect shown to it. It's a major problem. I'm surprised there aren't more jet-lag related accidents, she adds, and the room all purse their lips and exhale as if to say, right on doctor, you said it babe.

Deadpool says right, absolutely, and maybe we should set up a fund to research it some more but, in any event, the whole team are delighted you're back on your feet and you sure scared us there for a moment but heck you must be a tough cookie and they sure breed them tough here in Wales. We're also super grateful for all the help you gave the trust with the legal work over the years.

I half smile, feeling enormously self-conscious what with the cameraman and the other members of the film crew I've now noticed are loitering in the corner of the room trying to blend in with the surroundings, the off-white colour scheme, the shifting paintings on the Big TV, now a Banksy, now a Klimt.

Until you've been there, it's difficult to explain how this scenario unnerves you, makes you feel like you must think about every movement, blink, grimace, smile, frown. I couldn't be a celebrity if you paid me.

An envelope is handed to me.

"This is from me and Rob and Danny DeVito" says Deadpool.

"He's filming the 25th anniversary episode of Its Always Sunny in Philadelphia so can't be here today in person but he's joining us by video link."

On the screen of the Big TV, the heavily bearded face of Danny DeVito appears on one side of the screen with Deadpool and Rob McElhenney and a crazy looking version of me on an unlikely four-way split.

"Hey there" says Danny. "You scared us there for a while buddy" he says, laughing, pointing towards me. "Sorry I can't be with you today buddy, but as Ryan, sorry Deadpool, pointed out, I'm filming over here in Philly."

He scans the room behind him where the cast of Paddy's Bar are assembled wearing various Wrexham replica shirts from the 1978 title winning season, others from the 1990s and a special black version which I'm sure I once had. He brings the camera back on himself. "Great to have you back on board though. You sure did keep us on our toes."

"And it's always good to put to bed that potential manslaughter charge" laughs Deadpool.

"Yeah, we thought you were dead buddy, but turns out you were just having a nap."

"Yeah, a decade long nap."

"You lazy fuck" says Danny.

The whole room guffaws. Dr Paskin looks like she's going to come in her surgical knickers. It's amazing how some people command a room, have charisma, make people listen, laugh, influence the entire mood of a person, a room, a generation.

"Anyhow" says Rob, "potential incarceration and unwanted buggery in the showers aside, it's super-great to have you on your feet again."

Deadpool full on wallops me on the back. I shunt forward. I nearly went through a wall. He certainly packs a punch, this superhero.

"As you'll soon see, we've been pretty busy whilst you've been sleeping" says Rob, the comedian.

Deadpool laughs at this and says a quip that I don't quite hear but Dr Paskin looks like she's going for a multiple orgasm and the whole room is guffawing like there's no tomorrow.

I opened the envelope. It's an invite to play a lawyer in Deadpool 11. "It's only a small part, a couple of lines, but we thought it would be nice for you to have on your CV."

I'm overwhelmed. I'm handed a coat. It's one of those training ground efforts with my initials on the left, beneath the club crest. "Put it on Hun" says Deadpool, deadpan.

I put it on with the help of one of the crew. It's crazy how such a simple task takes on an altogether more complex angle when a camera crew is watching you. Maybe I've always had spatial awareness issues but who knew putting a jacket on could be such hard work. I get my arms in and straighten them out like you do when you try on a new garment.

"It looks wonderful" says Rob as Danny DeVito exits the screen, high fiving some man wearing a Ramones T-shirt, eating a sandwich in the background. I do what the satirical superhero says, and it fits glove-like. I feel special. I feel like a professional footballer, a celebrity, a somebody.

Dr Paskin leads the exit of the room. We funnel out into a series of corridors. I'm heading towards a glass door feeling like a salmon making its way home. The air, when you've been institutionalised for a decade is a weird thing to ingest, digest, consume. It has a sweet, floral almost nectar-like quality to it. My tongue feels sharp, taking it all in. The sounds are echoey, enhanced, as if this is all playing out through an other-worldly sound system.

My vision is making out clear, vivid lines on objects otherwise banal; benign branches on trees, the wings of seabirds yellow and grey against a bruised sky, buildings reflecting the clearest shards of glorious sunlight. I'm blindfolded and placed delicately into a car. The pattern of light shifts as my retina and cornea adjusts. The sense of colour fluctuates between a pale amber through to dark ox blood. It's beautiful watching this through my closed eyelids.

The engine starts up. There's a soft conversation between the driver and a passenger. There's no accent to detect, just a bland line of consonants and short vowels. The tone of the carriageway shifts from a rough highway, potholed probably (unless society has worked out a solution to alleviate this minor arse-ache) to a smooth almost unnoticeable tarmac.

On the radio, someone is talking about another assassination attempt on Trump. 'There's not much left of him,' comments the newsreader. Someone else mentions he is dead. A supporter saying 'fake news' and 'he's still relevant' is quickly drowned out by a sports bulletin; an absurdly handsome news anchor I imagine, following fixtures and tables and results that flash in strips around the edge of the screen - so much information, I wouldn't know where to look.

Then, a weather forecast, tightening isobars, a storm on its way. Storm Terry. Why the fuck would you call a storm, Terry? Tension in the Balkans. A light-hearted story about an old man running a marathon. A bit more about Trump, some old footage from a reality show. Reports about a Yeti sighting in Anglesey. Someone in Scotland claimed he saw the Loch Ness Monster in a pond outside Arbroath.

The engine disengages, the car coming to a halt. The clicking of a door handle, the door sliding open. An arm grips beneath mine and I instinctively half stand still within the car, which must be a people carrier or a large 4 X 4.

The senses, already spiked to fuck, really are trying to align, to take in the landscape, now a pale orange, as I'm led outside, my face still covered by some blindfold or balaclava.

A siren, coming closer, passing us now, probably a fire engine and I'm imagining a blaze in a factory; fireworks perhaps shooting off in different directions, a helicopter capturing this spectacular scene and filming it live across a news channel, across the edges of the screen, strips of weather forecast, stock indices, an Indonesian earthquake that is probably happening somewhere.

The wailing crescendos and then fades out, the sun emerging from a cloud, something almost spiritual about the shift in tone.

There's a sound now of birdsong, of background talk, the low tone of men's voices, some laughter, hard sounding consonants, drawn out echoing vowels. There's something about the heat that is different from before. It's somehow drier, harsher, sucking the air from your throat.

I need this thing to be removed. I'm suffocating here. Dr Paskin reassures me that the mask will be removed soon enough. It's right to feel nervous. It's a natural and ultimately positive reaction. It's all part of the journey.

Sure enough, somebody with smelly fingers, like diesel or cod liver oil, pulls the face mask off. I probably look like one of those Peruvian miners who come out after 300 days underground: eyes smarting, hands shielding retinas from the sunlight and the paparazzi flashlight.

The first thing you must comment on, is not the fact there's a man, a full-on Hollywood A-lister, dressed up as one of his characters, the spoof superhero Deadpool, or the fact there's a documentary crew zooming cameras, sound equipment in my direction, or even the crowd of thousands that appear spreading out along the avenue that heads towards the town centre.

No, even though you'd be ok thinking all that stuff is weird, what happens next is enough to really freak you out.

I'm standing in front of a football stadium that I've been to hundreds of times before, but the stadium is incredibly more modern than what I remember. The once derelict standing area known as the Kop is now a state-of-the-art stand, an incredible concourse, a museum, with the glorious Turf Pub incorporated into the scheme: I'm delighted they've retained some authenticity amidst the improvements. The only original stand I remember is on the Mold Road.

The melancholy is almost choking, an overwhelming flood of segments of time, moments beyond football but which always merged into the football of that time as if your life, the stuff that was happening then, was intrinsically wrapped up in whatever league you were in, how many goals your striker was scoring, the relative who died, the girl you were letting down gently whilst travelling to Port Vale away in the first round of the cup.

The walkway running past this new stand towards the town centre is swirling with red and white football shirts, scarves, flags, people wearing T-shirts with 'It's Always Sunny in Wrexham,' superhero face masks of the Deadpool character, other characters, some I recognise, some which have clearly been conceived during my coma-kip.

The road is pedestrianised and goes past a spanking new train station, off towards the town centre. Everything is different. The place feels energised. People are smiling. It really feels sunny here in Wrexham.

Deadpool stands before me. There's a huge crowd beyond the camera crew.

166

A chorus of "We love you Deadpool," comes from the crowd on an endless loop. The man in the superhero costume comes closer. The camera crew zooms in. The Superhero pulls up his face mask revealing the real-life face of the actor Ryan Reynolds. He grips my face with his two manly hands.

"Welcome to the 2030s" he says, gesturing towards the stadium.

"Take a look at this" says Ryan, now, absurdly dressed neck down as Deadpool, only his head exposed. The Hollywood hybrid embraces me, and Rob McElhenney appears on the other side wearing a vintage 1978 promotion shirt by Adidas.

"Well, what do you think of this then?" he says all deadpan, gently slapping my face, the cameraman zooming in close, capturing the three of us in an unlikely embrace.

"It was to be fair, Ryan's mistake" he says, turning to the camera, "he's never quite sure which side of the road it is over here."

I'm still not sure if they're joking with me; whether it was them who caused the coma or whether it was a fight in Scunthorpe or somebody taking me out at five a side. Ah well, I'm sure all will come out in good time.

The crowd, now sardined as a blur of red and white, into the walkway, makes the scene resemble a music festival or the inauguration of a president, erupt into a chorus of: "And it's Wrexham F.C., Wrexham F.C. are we. We're by far the greatest team, the world has ever seen."

Ryan and Rob turn to the crowd, me sandwiched in between them, and do that fake orchestra conductor thing people sometimes do, and they're gesturing for me to do the same, so I do, and the rendition grows louder and louder and then Ryan starts shouting: "Sheep, sheep, sheep, shaggers."

Further down the street, separated by a row, ten deep of police dressed like Robocops, are a sea of blue and white, Union Jacks, England flags, lots of youths wearing Stone Island, some other brands I don't recognise.

There're people in Wolverine masks, chanting. A man in his fifties with a tattoo on his face of the Incredible Hulk climbs up a lamp post and conducts the crowd. A rendition, of God Save The King echoes across the street, even though in 2030, they haven't got a king or a queen.

The Wrexham contingent respond by singing "Wrexham" over and over and another song questioning the lineage of the monarchy. The police hold the two sides together as a helicopter comes into view, dipping down low, in between the vast new floodlights of The Racecourse Ground.

A man dressed as Wolverine abseils down onto the roof of one of the stands from where he takes off a balaclava to reveal the actor and owner of F.C. Romans of Chester City (2023), Hugh Jackman.

The crowd, in a frenzy now, sing "you let your club die, you let your club die, you sad English bastards, you let your club die" and with the camera viewing the scene from behind us, the song continues for a good two to three minutes before Rob raises a finger to his lips and talking now into a microphone that has been passed to him, says a lingering "shush" to the crowd.

It takes perhaps half a minute for everyone to settle. Ryan grabs the microphone and points to the electronic hoarding on the corner of the new stand and the original stand on Mold Road, where I always sat: "Congratulations everybody. To the Newbies and especially to you The Lifers, this is for your years of dedication."

He points to the electronic scoreboard on the top of the New Kop. The floodlights of The Racecourse Ground loom like alien invaders from an HG Wells novel and throw out a triangle of brilliant white light, despite it being early afternoon on a beautiful summer's day, as if to show off the wonderful light show.

Then there's a blast of fireworks into the Wrexham sky, spectacular red and white rockets zooming above the stadium and the town.

I feel a pang of nostalgia. I remember people I have watched games with, segments of memories of goals scored, victories against all odds, gut-wrenching last-minute defeats.

The reality of what has happened during the last 10 years is displayed in electronic writing in vivid dragon red.

WELCOME TO THE CAE RAS
JUNE 20th, 2030
CHAMPIONSHIP PLAY-OFF FINAL
WREXHAM A.F.C. V F.C. ROMANS OF CHESTER CITY (2024)

The camera crew are focusing on Hugh Jackman, owner of Chester, still dressed as Wolverine who has abseiled down into the ground and is doing keep-me-ups in the centre circle of the pitch. Ryan and Rob are giving him wanker signs and then the international symbol for knob head from their vantage point. Danny DeVito is trying to get through the screen to give him a piece of his mind.

The police are pushing through to get the Chester supporters into the away section of the ground. It's carnage. It's everything that is wrong with society, humanity - the hatred, the vitriol, the nationalism, the tinges of racism that still swirl in the largely white population.

And it's also everything that is wonderful about the sport, about belonging, about supporting something that doesn't always provide you with much reward. There's something deeply exhilarating about the scene; my blood is pumping, my heart pounding. I feel energised. I feel fucking alive.

The crowd are herded into their respective areas. The stadium is full to its new capacity of 30,000. The play-off finals used to be at Wembley but now that's not possible, the Football Association decided to play it at whoever finished higher in the league. Wrexham finished third with Chester fifth, so the game was to be played in North Wales.

We settled down in our seats. There's Humphrey, me, my long-suffering life partner Sarah, my mum and dad, my boys, Ianto and Iolo, and Ryan and Rob. Behind us are their families, my buddies, Colin, Glyn, Stephen, Alan, and Jason and then my sister, brother-in-law, and nephews.

The players finish their warmups and disappear from the pitch down the tunnel into the changing rooms where they'll go through the last moment preparations, a final look at the marking plans for set pieces, a final brief team talk telling them not to leave anything out there.

The event is a blur, other-worldly. The noise is intense after a decade of deep coma-sleep. Chester fans go through their medley, and you can hear their collective accent of plastic Scouse, which I always find funny, how large crowds can create their dialect through shout and tune.

The rivalry has always been intense but it's up a notch. The implications and consequences of one of these clubs getting to the Premier League and conversely one failing is almost too much to comprehend.

There's a load of media stuff going on. The Netflix people keep zooming in on me and Ryan and Rob, sat each side of me, making small talk, wearing replica shirts, asking me stuff about the offside rule and the level of force permitted in a shoulder barge. Danny DeVito is also still there on screen, watching everything with an infectious energy.

Rob has a flag that he waves every now and then. There are some people I recognise amongst the crowd who I've seen over the forty odd years I've been supporting the club. I've seen people go through the cycle of life, families who have grown old together - babies, boys growing into men, middle age, death. And I must mirror them.

I ask Ryan his view on Man-Uggs. He says he didn't know it was a thing. I confirm it is a thing and that I recall having a pair, light camel coloured, came halfway up the shin, lined with fur. Beautiful to wear, an incredible level of comfort.

Humphrey says there's no room for debate, they're a 100 percent no go, absolutely should never be worn, even on the corpse of your worst enemy. I tell him to go fuck himself. He reverts with a wanker sign which is fair enough. Humphrey is cool. I like him. Intelligent and understated. A gentle wit.

I ask if anyone can remember the chocolate bar, Marathon. They all can. We agree, the rebrand to Snickers was nonsensical and the commercials with Mr. T from the A Team were truly horrific. I said I would never eat a Snickers just because the of the name and the commercial. And they used to be one of my favourites.

We discuss our Top 5 confectionary. Nutty Bar features, as does the Chunky Kit Kat and a Double Decker. Bounty gets a mention. As does the classic Mars Bar and Boost. We agree that a Yorkie Bar is a good allrounder.

The teams emerge from the tunnel. The atmosphere is like the biggest electric storm you've ever seen, in real life or on National Geographic. The stadium is like nothing I can remember ever witnessing. I am shaking. My words are coming out all wobbly. I started crying. I'm an emotional car crash. A lifetime of stuff is excreting from my body and face at just the wrong time. The documentary makers love it, I can feel the zoom on the camera across the stadium, getting right in on my tear-strewn face.

The game starts. Ryan and Rob are incredibly engaged. They seem almost obsessively terrified, every time the opposition goes near our goal and beside themselves whenever we attack the opposition. They're actors right, so there's a sceptical moment when I consider whether any of this is for the cameras, for the entertainment value, a business transaction, trying to sell stuff and whether they care. Is this fake, is it bullshit?

Ryan keeps saying "this is an anxiety circus." It's a weird thing to say but to be fair, it's not a bad description of the feeling that goes with being a supporter.

The quality of the football is in marked contrast to the stuff I recall being served up back in the non-league days, especially under Dean Keates. Don't get me wrong, he was a wonderful midfielder, one of the best in our recent history. Managerially, he gave everything, and like all things during that era, we were hamstrung by budget and limited skillsets by people who were

171

giving their best, on their own time, when most competitors had infrastructures, made up by paid up professionals, with a budget better than ours. Whether Dean Keates would have succeeded with a bigger budget and 'proper' infrastructure, will never be known.

We all think we can manage the club we support, and we don't see the players train, know what is going on behind the scenes, but in terms of mentality, the way a manager sets his team up tactically, is often a reflection of their own selves, the way they view the world, decide to live.

Some are conservative, play primarily not to lose, some work on the basis they want to simply score more than the opposition, with many being somewhere in the middle, like most spectrums. You can argue that it's easier when a club is properly resourced, and more so when a club is very well resourced, for a manager's tactical mentality to be more positive than when the club has scarce resources.

The football resembles that of continental Europe. It's slick and the ball is predominantly kept on the ground. It's difficult to get used to. I keep waiting for the thump up field.

There's a voice I recognise from where I used to sit. A real moaning bastard. He was old then, back in 2020, so he must be very old now. His voice is fainter and yet more moany. He's ironically telling our centre back, to 'get it forward.'

It appears some people still crave the days of kick and rush. There's no pleasing all the people, all the time, as someone more philosophical than me probably once said.

It's an interesting concept. Do some people, maybe not consciously, subliminally perhaps, prefer things to remain shit, to remain the way they were? They probably don't like mobile phones, or social media, or technology and only maybe realise some things are to be championed when they benefit, such as from a defibrillator at an event when struck by a sudden cardiac arrest, or a sat nav system finding the ground at Dagenham and Redbridge (don't bother by the way).

The first half plays out with Wrexham dominating the early possession, the goalkeeper, playing it short to one of the centre-backs, who then sweeps it across to one of the other centre-backs, who then play it out to the wing-backs who run forward, then play it in field to one of the centre-midfielders who then play a ball up to the forwards and so it goes.

Chester presses high and hard. Their supporters sing the national anthem which still sounds weird with the word 'King' in it. They wave union jacks with a fervour and an aggression, and the chill of imperialism and conquest fills the air.

The passion and fanaticism that comes with football when it spills over into a completely different creature can be ugly and dangerous to watch. Despite the local rivalry, when you watch the opposing supporters and the bitterness and hate that spill back and forth, it's the really disgusting side of football. Whether this kind of behaviour would exist attached to a different vehicle if football didn't exist, we can only speculate.

Against the run of play, Chester scores on the break. A long goal kick from veteran goalkeeper Jordan Pickford and Flint born Barry Rush, no relation by all accounts to Ian, despite him having quite a nose and purportedly being quite well endowed, like his famous namesake.

Wrexham continued to play neat, measured football but Chester defended stoically. In the last minute, a through ball from local boy Jordan Davies, and veteran record goal scorer for Wrexham, Paul Mullin, now 36 years old, lobs the goalkeeper with a typically deft finish.

The stadium erupts and the game goes into extra time, a typically cagey affair with nobody wanting to make a mistake. Inevitably the game ends as a draw and the lottery of a penalty shootout looms. The drama of a penalty shootout cannot be conveyed in the written word. It's an absurd finale to a game of sport where an entire season is decided on such a lottery.

Each player scores their penalty. It keeps going. One after the other, coolly slotted into the net in front of the Wrexham fans and the New Kop. It gets to the point where every outfield player has scored. It comes down to the goalkeepers. It's brutal; whoever misses loses and the season is over, and their club remains in the Championship, with the victor promoted to the Premier League, the elite football league in the entire world.

Jordan Pickford steps up for Chester. The ball wobbles on its spot. He walks back to re-spot it. He looks sideways to the referee who seems to hold her whistle in her mouth for a lifetime. Everything seems to be moving in slow motion. The images of the crowd, the managers, the players, everything stands still for the moment.

He steps up and hits the ball as hard as he can. Ben Foster, 47 years old, still agile, still charismatic, going down to his right, produces an incredible save, reminiscent of the save he made in that pivotal victory against Notts County in 2023.

He leaps up and salutes the crowd and then suddenly cuts short his celebration, perhaps realising that the job is not yet done. He has a penalty to take, to win the match, to win promotion, to get Wrexham to the Premier League for the first time in its 166-year history.

He steps up, takes off his absurdly large gloves. He looks to the New Kop beyond the goal. He takes in the moment, concentrates on images in the crowd; a young boy being held by his father, an elderly woman leaning against a frame, groups of friends stood in an embrace.

There're people looking the other way, their hands held up to a higher force, willing for this to go their way. There're are a million thoughts going through his head. This is history in the making. This moment in time will affect so many lives, so many people. It's a massive responsibility.

He takes a deep breath, spots the ball. He doesn't look at the referee. He runs up and smashes it high into the top corner.

Wrexham won.

Wrexham are in the Premier League.

Fucking hell.

The referee decked out in an orange kit, tattoos submerging her arms and legs and neck, cutting a fearful character, blows her whistle, signaling the contest is over.

The scoreboard and the electronic hoardings around the pitch declare WREXHAM ARE IN THE PREMIER LEAGUE. We're promoted. We're in the Premier League. You could say it out loud, over, and over, whisper it to yourself, shout it from the peak of a mountain, say it internally; whichever format you might use, it doesn't make any sense. It's illogical, it's absurd.

In sporting terms (why, do I always have to caveat the feeling of euphoria when talking about football, to reflect perhaps that I understand there are bigger issues in life – illness, poverty, an earthquake that will be playing out somewhere), this is the apex, the summit.

Years of decay, deterioration, disintegration, awful asset-stripping capitalists trying to pilfer the spirit a community have built up, pooled within, magma seeping beneath the plates of a mountain, spilling out through the fissures of a volcano. There's a collective eruption of joy, years of pent-up pressure suddenly vented into a cloud of sheer euphoria.

I look around the stadium, the people on the pitch. There are people I've seen every other week for many years and have never spoken to. A nod here and there. A gesture. A shake of the head, a thumbs up. There's a feeling of solidarity and community being a supporter of a football club. And maybe this is stronger when you're in the lower leagues? Does it diminish if you become successful? Will other football fans now despise us?

They're all questions I wouldn't have dreamt of even thinking a decade before when we were floundering in the fifth tier and to be honest, I don't really care - we've done our time, we deserve this.

I liken us to that band who have toured the pubs and clubs for years and

175

then get their big record deal, their chance at the big time. We're not a Forest Green or a Salford, without a history, a tradition, an embedment in the local community, and who are always susceptible to their owners growing tired, bored, or losing their personal wealth.

We have a substance, a soul, an authenticity, a connection with the locality, the community, a proud principality, and that was part of the reason why Ryan and Rob decided to buy the club in the first place.

I could stand and watch this scene forever. It's staggering, gorgeous, insane, it might sound melodramatic but after the birth of my kids, this is one of the most memorable moments of my life.

I concentrate on the row of poplar trees beyond the stand opposite, their silver-green leaves shimmering on the summer breeze. They've been a constant since I first came here back in the 1970s; a source of comfort, normality, a backdrop to whatever is happening in my life at that snapshot of time and whatever is happening on the football pitch beyond it.

Football is a tribal thing. There's so much of it I despise. The greed, the money, the lack of loyalty, the histrionics by players as they attempt to win fouls and free kicks. It's something however that, if you're conceived into a football family, you don't really have a choice. It's in your blood, in your heart, in your soul, it's part of your DNA.

I often think what would have happened back in the 1970s if my dad had carried on down the motorway towards England and the hotbed of top league football in Manchester and Liverpool instead of turning off to Wrexham. The link is that fickle.

There are times when I wish he hadn't, but moments like these when supporting a club starved of success, means so much. For all that disappointment, the defeat, the struggle, it makes this moment feel more noble, more deserving. It's difficult to articulate.

It's a strange feeling, sitting there, watching my team getting promotion to the Premier League. That emotion when you fulfill a dream, the girl you fancied across the dance floor back in the day, the car, the promotion, the healing of an illness. It's overwhelming.

All that shit that you think is everything when you're younger. And you sit there and enjoy the moment and you want so much for it to stay there forever, to press pause, to stay in the moment just for a little longer.

There're people on the pitch, dancing around, waving flags, the stench of smoke grenades fills the air. I try and process this emotion. I want to drink it in, let it soak through me.

A woman approaches me, dressed in a Paddy Power uniform. She has a soft Dublin accent. I recognise it from somewhere in my history.

"Congratulations" she says "your bet came in; we've transferred the winnings, £1million into your account. The double you put on back in 2020 came in."

Fuck me.

So, I remain in my seat for a good hour after the final whistle. The documentary people I notice are taking a shot from across the stadium, an arty close-up of me looking all euphoric for the achievement, and yet melancholic for the past and those who have gone before us and haven't been able to witness this absurdity; the documentary maker loves an emotional paradox.

Some players are warming down, dressed in skin-tight super-Lycra, a modern fabric designed to make you slightly better than the other team who can't afford such luxuries. It's a strange place, a football stadium, when it's empty: something cathedral about it, almost spiritual, and I'm not a religious man.

Rob and Ryan stand and gesture for me to remain in my seat, as they follow the celebrities exiting the Director's Box. Presidents Zelenskyy and Gorbachev, Spencer Harris, Joe Wicks, Madonna, A.L.F., Michael Sheen, Rob Brydon, Bootlegger, Bryn Law, Tom Jones, Gareth Bale, Fizz from

Coronation Street, manager of Premier League Walsall, Dean Keates, Steve Massey-Ferguson, Derek the Weatherman, Huw from BBC News, Mike Peters, his wife Jules, my mates Glyn, Stephen, Colin, Alan and Jason, all disappearing down the steps, enjoying their day out at the hottest ticket in town.

They understand the need for some solace, some time to reflect or they recognise it's a good bit of footage for the documentary; they're actors, so, who knows. Ryan, empathetic super-hero that he is, asks if I'm alright.

"Everything ok buddy?"

"Thinking you're going to miss playing Boreham Wood and Ebbsfleet every week?" chips in Rob.

"Scared of a crowd" laughs Danny DeVito.

"Afraid the big grounds won't let you in wearing your shitty Crocs?" guffaws Ryan.

"Or your fucking god-awful Man-Ugg's" chortles Rob.

"Surprised you're not wearing one of your collection of shirts from the eighties, to show what a loyal supporter you were" laughs Danny.

I lift my 2030 shirt, with WORLD PEACE on the front, beneath it a T-shirt with WHERE WERE YOU WHEN WE WERE SHIT emblazoned across it.
There'll always be a slight, mostly subliminal, feeling for the long-standing supporter that we were there when things weren't so glamorous, the games against places that you swear were made up. The 'Lifers' as Ryan calls us.

The overwhelming emotion from the more rational supporter is, however, to embrace the revolution, to welcome those who have joined the cause of this great football club, (unless they steal your seat, or get the last tray of chips (for a quid?)).

Rob and Ryan give me a half-hug each which I suppose adds up to one whole hug and Danny weighs in with a virtual high five and they disappear down the staircase, leaving me alone, a feeling of nostalgia, of being soaked in the sweat and tears of my past, a forgotten history, drowning in the dark tide of failings, defeats, fractured dreams, people who have fallen out of my life, things I would have done differently, things I wouldn't have changed for the world.

It sounds absurd but it's difficult watching a dream come true, something you've yearned for all your life. You're told from an early age to dream big, from the trophies on your early bedspreads, the posters on your walls, as life only loves and remembers a winner, right? Well, you're that winner now, you've achieved what you've always dreamed of.

Beyond the stadium and the floodlights, beneath the glorious rolling Welsh countryside of hills and fields, I watch the last of the crowd snaking down Mold Road and through the grid of familiar surrounding streets and amidst the sea of faces, there's Spidermen, Deadpool's and Wolverines, some Hulks, that wayward Zippy from Rainbow, draped in Stone Island, and Armani, threatening to skirmish.

Amidst the sound of euphoria, a collective song of joyous voice hanging in the summer sky, a full red sun arcing beyond the stadium, above the distant purple hills, the sky taking on a golden shade, the evening drenched in warm amber sunshine, and as dusk falls, the sky, is a million shades of beautiful Wrexham Red.

ABOUT THE AUTHOR

Andrew Foley Jones is a lawyer and a writer/columnist for a number of publications. A lifelong Wrexham AFC fan and previously the lawyer for the club, pre-take over, this is his hilarious part fact/fiction take on recent events in his native North Wales.

COYR

IANTO GRYFF

IOLO BERA

SFJ

Printed in Great Britain
by Amazon

30682588R00104